W9-BRD-414

Self-reliance

Recession-proof your pantry

A self-reliance guide from Backwoods Home Magazine

Contributors — *Jackie Clay, Jeffrey R. Yago, Sylvia Gist, Linda Gabris*

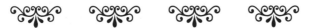

ISBN 978-0-9821577-3-2

Backwoods Home Publications
www.backwoodshome.com

Edited by Ilene Duffy, Rhoda Denning, and Lisa Nourse
Drawings by Don Childers

Contents

The Pantry

Canning

Drying, Smoking, & Pickling Foods

A self-reliance guide from Backwoods Home Magazine

The Pantry

"It is thrifty to prepare today for the wants of tomorrow."
from The Ant and the Grasshopper

Long-term food storage

By Jackie Clay

You've decided that you're going to put at least a year's worth of food away for your family just in case. Great!

Everyone should do that. We store enough to feed friends, extended family, and neighbors from time to time, as well. We could not turn down anyone who came to us saying, "I'm hungry." So I stock up more than most people do.

Flours and grains

Man may not live by bread alone, but grains form the base for many meals, especially during a period of hard times. With flours and whole grains stored, you have the main ingredient for homemade pastas, breads, rolls, biscuits, pancakes, waffles, tortillas and other flat breads, pie crusts, cookies, cakes, and more.

I store unbleached (who needs bleaching compounds in their diet?) flour, at least 200 pounds, in 25-pound store bags, wrapped in plastic bags and duct tape, in Rubbermaid garbage cans with locking lids in my pantry. This will feed three of us, plus extra for friends and family, for over a year, coupled with other flour products and whole grains.

You can add any specialty flours your family likes, such as rye, amaranth, or Durham (for specialty pastas).

In addition to this flour, I like at least 100 pounds of hard wheat (sometimes called "wheat berries"). As ground whole wheat goes rancid fairly quickly, I like this wheat on hand to grind for all of my whole wheat recipes. In addition, whole wheat grain will grow when planted, making wheat growing on a fairly small plot possible to restock my supply. As little as a 50x50-foot plot will grow enough wheat for a small family's needs.

I also stock about 20 pounds of cornmeal, 20 pounds of masa harina de maize (corn flour) which I use to make tamales and corn tortillas, along with 25 pounds of popcorn (grinds nicely for cornmeal, as well as popping for treats), and 25 pounds of hominy corn (makes hominy and also masa harina de maize).

Rice, both brown and white, fit nicely in our storage pantry. We also store about 25 pounds of a combination of white and brown rice with a few pounds of wild rice mixed in.

And don't forget rolled oats. They are much more versatile than just using them for oatmeal. I include them in several multi-grain breads, breakfast cake, bars, meat loaf, granola, and cookies. And as for oatmeal, we like it cooked up with peaches, strawberries, and apples with cinnamon for a treat.

Any grains that are ground, especially cornmeal, masa harina de maize, and whole wheat will get rancid quicker than do whole grains, which usually stay good for many years. Even so, flours (except whole wheat flour) will stay perfectly good for five years or more if kept dry and stored in airtight and bug and rodent-proof containers.

I buy my white flour, cornmeal, etc. on sale at local supermarkets, usually just before Thanksgiving, as it is cheaper then. Otherwise, I pick it up at Sam's Club or other restaurant supply houses.

I pick up whole grains from local grain farmers. Sometimes the

Home canning helps fill the pantry. Note decorative popcorn tins in the background, filled with dry foods.

wheat needs a bit more cleaning if dusty, but a few pours from one basket to another on a windy day ensures very clean wheat. (And my wheat is *not* treated with toxic fumigants in storage bins before being ground into flour, as is most wheat sold to flour mills.)

When buying flour to store, be absolutely sure the bags are completely sealed, with no flour leaking out, to prevent flour weevil problems. In areas where there is a weevil problem (webs and "bugs" in unsealed cornmeal and flour), some folks freeze each bag of flour for several days before wrapping and storing it in completely bug-proof containers. I have not done this, but I am exceptionally careful not to store any flour products that were not very well sealed from the processing plant, and I keep them in insect-proof containers. Remember that these moths are very small and squeeze through very tiny openings.

It is not necessary to buy flours and grains from long-term storage companies unless you fear flooding. In this case, sealed tins or buckets of flours would be a good idea. I've had plain white flour stored for over five years, which is just as good today as it was when I bought it.

Beans and other legumes

When one thinks of long-term storage, usually dried beans come first to mind. I guess this is because they remain good for so long, are nutritious, and taste pretty darned good to boot. But, for heaven's sake, don't just buy a hundred pounds of navy beans and say you're all set for whatever may come your way. All beans do not taste the same. There's a big, big difference between a large white lima and a Jacob's cattle bean, for instance. Some taste nutty, some bland. Some cook up quickly, some require hours of cooking. Some remain firm after cooking, others get mushy and soft. Experiment with a wide variety of beans before committing to a choice.

We store about 50 pounds of combined legumes, which include pintos, Cherokee mixed cornfield beans, Jacob's cattle, Hopi black bush, navies, red kidney, and a dozen old Native American varieties, along with lentils, soup peas, black-eyed peas, and garbanzos.

Beans are a great protein source and combine well in many different dishes. Refried beans, fried dry pea patties, stews, soups, chiles, baked beans, and casseroles are just a few uses for these versatile legumes. You can buy your beans in local markets, health food stores, and co-ops, or you can do like we do, and grow your own.

All beans store a long, long time in an airtight and bug and rodent-proof container. I keep mine in gallon glass jars and in decorative popcorn tins, right on handy shelves in the kitchen. While old beans do take longer to cook up tender, they last indefinitely; I've grown beans from 500-year-old seeds. And if you can grow plants from seed, you can certainly eat them.

Dried pasta

While I make a lot of homemade pasta, I still keep quite a bit in our storage pantry. When you're busy with a survival situation, you may not have time to make pasta. So I've put away 10 pounds of long spaghetti, 10 pounds of lasagna noodles, 10 pounds of wide egg noodles, 5 pounds of alphabet macaroni, 15 pounds of elbow macaroni, and a few pounds of assorted pasta noodles.

This dry pasta keeps indefinitely when stored in a dry, bug and rodent-proof container. As with my beans and other legumes, I use decorative popcorn tins and gallon glass jars.

Sugar and honey

You will probably agree with me that we all eat too much sugar. And although honey is natural and better for us than refined sugar, it's still sugar. But in bad times, we usually feel better with "treats" from time to time. And these treats often include sugar. Also, much fruit is home canned with a sugar syrup, and if you're going to can to keep your pantry from running out in bad times, you'll need quite a bit for fruits, pickles, jams, jellies, preserves, etc.

Although my husband Bob is a diabetic, we do include sugar in our storage pantry. I keep a 25-pound sack in a plastic garbage can, along with assorted other dry foods. Much of this sugar is used in canning and desserts for my son, David, and myself. Bob needs a sugar substitute. Sugar stores indefinitely if kept dry. If it should get damp and harden, you can still save it. Beat the bag with a hammer, being careful not to split the sack. (I would put the paper bag in a heavy plastic bag, just in case.) Soon the hard lump will be many smaller ones, easy to crumble with your hand.

Honey is a good long-term storage bet. I keep two gallons of honey, stored in quart jars. Honey may crystallize if it gets too cool, but it is still good and will re-liquify if warmed up by sitting the jar in a saucepan of boiling water. Raw honey only needs to be put into quart or larger jars and sealed. I have 15-year-old honey that's still great. (In case you're wondering, I try to keep a little of each food for a long, long time, to see just *how* long it will remain good. I *do* rotate my long-term storage food, using the oldest and replacing it with newer food in an ongoing process.)

Besides these two sweeteners, I keep 10 pounds of brown sugar and 5 pounds of powdered sugar, stored in the bag they come in until I'm ready to use them. These bags are stored in the plastic garbage can, along with the white sugar and much more. The only problem I've had regularly with brown sugar is hardening in the bag. I've cured this by breaking the sugar into chunks, dropping them into a gallon glass jar and adding a piece of paper towel, dampened with water. Close the jar and in a few days the sugar will be soft again.

Miscellaneous dry goods

Powdered egg is a handy dry food to keep on the pantry shelves. The modern powdered egg is much better than the old "green eggs" of military service days. Not only is it great in cooking, but it tastes pretty good too. I keep three #10 cans, which hold almost a gallon, on my pantry shelves.

Powdered margarine and butter are another "must have" for most families. These are reconstituted with either water or vegetable oil, with

11

the oil tasting much better. I keep three of each, even though we have a cow and goats. One never knows when they may be dry and you need butter.

Powdered cheese is a great product that stores easily. I use it in macaroni and cheese, on popcorn, in potatoes au gratin, casseroles, and more. I keep about 10 pounds of a powdered cheese sauce that I buy from a local restaurant supply house quite inexpensively.

Dry yeast is a definite must in a long-term storage pantry, as well as in everyday use. I buy mine in 1-pound vacuum packed aluminum foil bags. Unopened and frozen, they last indefinitely. Unopened and on the shelf, they'll last for a couple of years. Opened and on the shelf, dry yeast is active for about a year or a little more. I keep an unopened bag in my propane fridge's freezer, figuring that if an emergency situation occurs, causing us to have to do without the fridge, my yeast will still be good for better than a year. I have another one on the shelf that I use every day.

Baking soda is also a necessary baking leavening agent, also useful for an antacid, deodorant, cleaner, and more. It keeps on the shelf forever. I keep 5 pounds.

Baking powder is hard to do without. You'll need it for quick breads, such as corn bread and biscuits, which are very important in emergencies because you can eat well and spend only minutes in baking. It keeps well for years without losing its leavening ability. I keep two large tins, one to use and one to store.

Salt is needed, not only to improve the flavor of foods but in meat preservation and canning. I keep 10 pounds of iodized salt in 1-pound boxes, and 10 pounds of canning salt. Canning salt is used in pickles because table salt contains chemicals that sometimes cause pickles to soften or discolor. Dry salt will keep forever. If it should harden, beat it with a hammer and it will be made useable.

Dry milk is a necessity, even for those of us who have dairy animals. One never knows when your animals may be dry and you need milk...*today*. Dehydrated milk does *not* taste as good as fresh. But it is great for cooking and it will work on cereal or for chocolate milk. The boxes at your local store will last for years with no change in taste. I keep about 10 pounds of dry milk, even though we have dairy animals. **Spices** are indispensable. Be sure to store a wide variety of your favorites. True, spices do lose some of their flavor in a year or so. But better to have an old spice than no spice. They will "keep" forever, but will slowly lose their potency. I buy most of mine in oriental markets and restaurant supply houses.

Miscellaneous canned necessities

Peanut butter isn't just for kids, folks. It's a tasty, great protein source that's versatile, as well. No one guesses that the secret ingredient in my best stir-fry is a tablespoonful of chunky peanut butter. Remember that besides peanut butter sandwiches and spread on toast, you can bake cookies and other desserts with this protein-filled treat. Unopened, it'll last for years.

Shortening and **vegetable oils** will make cooking more of a pleasure, not to mention all the baking you may want to do. Most shortenings will store indefinitely in the pantry and unopened bottles of vegetable oils will be fine for over a year, usually longer. Rotate the oils more frequently than the solid shortening. You will probably like using corn oil to reconstitute your powdered margarine and butter, instead of water. You'll use more shortening and vegetable oil in a year than you'd guess. I store a dozen cans of shortening and 6 large bottles of vegetable oil.

Dehydrated foods

Unless you need sealed cans of dehydrated foods, you can dehydrate food for long-term storage yourself. It's amazing how easy it is to dry foods at home. While I homecan a huge variety of foods, I also rely on dehydrated foods, which complement the canned foods. For instance, canned peas taste like nasty mush. Sorry, Jolly Green, it's the truth. So

13

instead of canning my peas, I dehydrate them. When rehydrated, they taste almost as good as fresh.

What foods can you dehydrate? Here is just a sample: raisins, cherries, pineapple, peaches, apples, plums, watermelon, peas, corn, hominy, beans, tomatoes, onions, potatoes, peppers, squash, pumpkin, apricots, mushrooms, asparagus, turnips, rutabagas, raspberries, blueberries, citrus peel, bananas, mangos, fruit leathers of all types and mixtures, and jerky. Gee, I get hungry just making this list.

Canned foods

While you can buy up a bunch of canned meats, vegetables, fruits, jams, jellies, pickles, and so forth at the store to put in a long-term storage pantry, it's a good idea to learn to homecan foods. Both will have an indefinite shelf life, but homecanned foods will be much more tasty and nutritious. And if a situation develops where you can not buy more storebought food, you can reuse your jars and rings (not lids) and homecan more food to restock your pantry. All it takes is a garden and a little skill.

Here are some samples of home canned foods you can store and use: apples, applesauce, apricots, baby foods, asparagus, barbecue sauces, beans of all types, beef roasts, stew meat, beets, blackberries, cabbage, corn, carrots, celery, cherries, cheese, chicken, chili, clam chowder, clams, conserves, corned beef, crab apple jelly & pickles, cranberry sauce, elderberry jelly, elk, fish, grapefruit, grapes, grape jelly, greens, jams, ground beef, jellies, juices, lamb, maple syrup, mixed vegetables, mincemeat, moose, mushrooms, okra, parsnips, peaches, pears, peppers, pickles, pie fillings, plums, plum jelly and conserve, poke, pork, potatoes, poultry, preserves, pumpkin, rabbit, raspberries, rhubarb, salsa, sauerkraut, sausage, seafoods, soups, taco meat, taco sauce, tomatoes, tomato catsup, tomato sauce, turkey, turnips, venison, watermelon pickles, wild game, fowl, and much more.

Remember though, there are 52 weeks in a year, so if times get tough you will need more food than you first think. There may be no fast food, only homecooked meals. Calculate carefully and err on the bountiful side, rather than have your family go hungry. And can a wide variety. No family likes to eat beans every meal.

Pet foods

Perhaps the easiest foods to store for your dogs and cats are dry foods. Under decent storage conditions, a good quality dog or cat food will remain fresh for at least a year. Store a high quality dry food, not the "cheaper" brands. As with most everything, you get what you pay for. Add up what your pets eat in a week, a month, then multiply it by 12. Store in rodent-proof containers.

It's also a good idea to include a few cans of quality dog and cat food for a treat now and then. I knew a lady who survived the depression with her dear fox terrier. The woman was very poor and could not afford any dog food, whatsoever. And, of course, there were very few table scraps. So to feed her beloved pet, she trapped woodchucks and muskrats, which she skinned for a few dollars and canned the boned meat for her dog. Coupled with a few meager table scraps, her fox terrier came through the hard times fat and sassy.

You and your family can come through hard times in triumph, not merely "survive" them. All it takes is a bit of planning, a lot of hard work, and some ingenuity. ◆

Can you survive out of your pantry for a whole year?

By Jeffrey R. Yago

Over the years I have provided many articles on emergency preparedness, and several included emergency food suggestions. However, these were easy-to-prepare instant meals for your vehicle, bug-out-bag, or home to get you through a week without power or groceries. These short-term problems could be due to an extended power outage, winter storm, or being stranded after a vehicle breakdown. Since these events could require moving to a safer area, the foods I chose for these emergencies are highly concentrated, lightweight, and can be packed into a relatively small storage box or backpack.

For these applications, it is also important to minimize meal preparation requirements, so most of these food items are dehydrated or powdered and can be easily reconstituted by adding a cup of hot water. Camping stores also offer individual meal packs that provide more variety and better taste, but these can cost more than $5 per single serving and do not have a long shelf life.

What about a long-term event that disrupts all food distribution in your area? What if you were unable to work or were in a disaster area and your rural area has minimum emergency support? With New Orleans and Katrina still fresh in most people's minds, this may not be an unrealistic possibility to worry about these days. What if a really catastrophic natural or man-made disaster affected your entire town or state, and it might take a year to reestablish any normalcy for trans-

16

portation, food distribution, and utilities? Yes, it is possible to remain in your own home and live fairly comfortably for many months without running to the grocery store each week, but eating small packs of stored instant noodles or Vienna sausages and crackers is not going to do it.

To prepare for a really long-term period of self-sufficiency, you need a supply of food that is very close to your normal diet, and not instant meals full of preservatives, chemicals, and sodium. Our bodies need a balanced input of fruits, vegetables, and protein, and a major change in your diet can affect your weight, disposition, and health.

To provide months of real food for emergencies you need a well-stocked pantry, but this is not your mother's pantry. This requires a large cool and dry storage space, and the regular task of rotating items to keep everything fresh. For example, if you cook one can of green beans each week, a year's supply for you would require two 24-can cases. If we add corn, peas, and other canned vegetables and fruits, you can see how your long-term pantry would soon take over most of the garage and would look like the corner store.

A serious long-term pantry will require sturdy shelving with easy access to both the front and back if possible. Recently purchased cans are added at the rear and older cans are moved forward to be used first. Keep a felt-tip marker pen by the pantry door and write the date on each new can. If rear access is not possible, always add to the back to keep the older dates towards the front.

The easiest way to get started in bulk food purchasing is to join a discount warehouse store where everything is sold by the case or in bulk containers. Each week select one specific vegetable or fruit and try to purchase one or more cases. After several months of this quantity shopping you should have at least a six-month's supply of each. If space allows, you can continue and build up a year's supply if desired. Since all canned products have a limited shelf life, it may not be possible to rotate more than a six-month supply without items going out-of-date, so watch the expiration dates printed on each can. By watching for specials and realizing some foods are more plentiful and lower cost at certain times of the year, your bulk purchases will be able to take advantage of these sales.

Many of you already have a garden and fruit trees and you can your own homegrown fruits, jellies, and garden vegetables, so you are already familiar with this process. This is an excellent way to have more nutritional canned fruits and vegetables for your pantry then you can buy at the local supermarket. A well-tended garden will also provide fresh items at least part of the year that will not require canning.

Although a large pantry will solve a big part of your long-term food storage requirements, we can't just eat everything from a can each day. Your normal daily diet also includes bread products, fresh meats, and hopefully fresh greens, and these food groups do not come in a can.

Grain mill a must

In addition to a long-term food storage there are two other things you absolutely must have—bulk wheat and a wheat mill. We take it for granted every time we grab a loaf of bread and a half gallon of milk on our way home from work, but what if the food supply chain is interrupted for any reason? Bread and milk are the first things to disappear from store shelves, and they can only stay fresh for a few days. If you check around the next time you are at the grocery store, there are no cases of food in a back room. All food items are now ordered by bar code and computers every few days, and are constantly arriving each week. What you see is all there is going to be if the distribution system is interrupted.

Raw wheat, if kept dry and free of insects, can last hundreds of years without any loss of quality or taste. Unfortunately, once wheat is ground into flour, it will only last a few days without turning rancid, which is why regular store-purchased flour is heavily bleached and full of preservatives. In fact, rodents will not touch bleached white flour. Yes, you will want a few bags of name-brand flour in your pantry, but this will not last long when you start baking your own bread and biscuits every few days. On the other hand, it takes very little wheat to make a lot of flour, and unlike packaged flour, fresh wheat flour is full of gluten and other natural nutrients your body needs.

Any long-term food pantry should have a supply of both red and winter-white wheat, which are usually sold in bulk 5-gallon plastic pails. These pails have all of the oxygen removed prior to sealing by purging with dry nitrogen. This kills all microscopic insects that may have entered during harvesting and packaging. Your pantry should also include several 5-gallon pails of hard corn (popcorn). Your wheat grinder can easily turn hard corn into cornmeal for frying fish or baking corn bread.

You can buy a hand-operated wheat grinder for very little cost, but believe me, it takes lots of cranking to make a cup of flour. If you have a backup source of emergency power, you should purchase an electric grain mill. Although they are not cheap, they are much better suited for regular use. The better models include covers with filters to eliminate flour dust, and have adjustable grinding sizes to quickly switch from wheat, barley, or corn.

If events require you to be on your own much longer than anticipated and you are forced to start baking from scratch on a regular basis, there are several other cooking ingredients besides flour you should have on hand and these are also some of the first items that will disappear from the store shelves. Refrigerated milk, butter, and eggs will not keep long, although you can freeze butter. These products are also available in bulk cans, but I'm not talking about WWII powdered eggs. Today, these everyday necessities are specially freeze-dried prior to canning, and will turn back into the original form in both taste and consistency when you add water. Unfortunately, like the bulk wheat mentioned above, you will not find these freeze-dried products at the local supermarket, so they will need to be ordered. Internet and mail order sources for these products are listed in the sidebar at the end of this chapter.

About every five years I reorder a few cans of freeze-dried foods, and I recently discovered several cans which are now 10 years old.

Normally I would consider this past the shelf life for even the specially-packaged freeze-dried products, but I decided to test them for this article before discarding. I opened nitrogen-packed 1-gallon cans of freeze-dried pure butter, whole milk, cheese, and ripe tomatoes. Each can contained a colorful dry powder, with the consistency of flour. I took a cupful of each separately and added an equal amount of water and after a little stirring I suddenly had real dairy butter and cheese, and a thick tomato paste.

Each tasted like they were fresh from the store, and the tomato paste had a very fresh tomato aroma. By varying the amount of water, you can make the cheese taste stronger or milder, and after a night in the refrigerator the butter and cheese became just as solid as they would have been to start with.

I then tried this test with several 3-year-old dehydrated meals you find in sealed foil pouches at most camping stores. After adding hot water I found these meals tasted very old and stale. For really long-term food storage necessities, I strongly recommend freeze-dried foods in nitrogen-packed cans. Most distributors use 1-gallon size cans with a special coating on the inside to reduce any metallic taste, and they add several oxygen-absorbing pouches just before sealing to remove any remaining oxygen.

After establishing your own reliable long-term supply of canned fruits and vegetables, and adding the ability to turn wheat into fresh bread products, most non-vegetarians will want to have meat for at least a few meals each week. It is possible to store a few canned hams or other canned meat products, but these are full of preservatives and still will have a relatively-short shelf life.

If possible, your long-term food program should include a good quality top-load freezer, and a way to keep it powered during a long-term power outage. I have provided several articles in past issues on solar-powered appliances and refrigerators and freezers. This might be a good time to review these articles to see if one might be right for you.

A frozen turkey can provide meat for up to a week when thawed and cooked. The same is true for a large beef or pork roast if you have the means to keep a freezer operating. You should also have a good supply of smaller frozen whole chickens, steaks, and fish. Be sure to clearly mark the date each was purchased and rotate on a regular basis with your normal meals. Most frozen meats should be eaten within six months.

All long-term food pantries need to include other incidentals you use on a regular basis, and these can be purchased in bulk to reduce space and cost. These will include salt, pepper, cinnamon, and any other favorite cooking spices. You will also need cooking oil or shortening, rice, dried beans of various types, powdered milk, baking soda, yeast, sugar, cornstarch, vinegar, and baking powder.

There are many incidental non-food items that are easy to store and will come in very handy during hard times. Bulk packages of plastic wrap, paper towels, plastic trash bags, toilet paper, matches, disposable plates and cups, powdered flavored drinks, tea, coffee, cocoa, and block chocolate make life much more civilized.

I am only addressing how to start your own long-term food storage in this article. However, being prepared to switch to a self-sufficient lifestyle, either by choice or under duress, requires other long-term preparations as well. Don't forget first-aid and medical needs, security needs, and personal hygiene needs, and these products will also require storage space and planning.

No one ever expects a disaster will involve them, yet every day the news reports some major storm or catastrophic event that forced hundreds and sometimes thousands of people to be stranded and on their own. At a time when most hurried families pick up what they plan to eat that night on their way home from work, many homes and apartments have less than three days of food on hand. Even fewer will have a way to prepare and cook these foods if the power fails.

You also need several gallons of fresh water each day, and municipal water supplies quickly become contaminated during times of disaster.

Unless you have an alternate means for electrical power, well pumps do not pump water if there is a power outage, so don't forget to keep as many gallons of water on hand that you have space for.

Having a month's supply of your everyday food in a nearby pantry and a year's supply of bulk-type emergency food provides real peace of mind. After all, maybe not your parents, but I guarantee your grandparents were able to eat very healthy meals each day without running to the corner store each evening.

Perhaps it's time to realize that although frozen foods and drive-through restaurants are really convenient, we all have become far too dependent on others for our everyday living. Having a well-stocked pantry is your first step to true independent living. 🦴

Sources for freeze-dried foods and supplies:

www.survivalcenter.com
360-458-6778

Freeze-dried Foods:
www.frontiersurvival.net
5765 Hwy. 64
Farmington, NM 87401
505-947-2200

www.survivalacres.com
800-681-1057

The Emergency Preparedness Center
www.areyouprepared.com
520 C. North Main St. Ste. 202
Heber City, UT 84032
435-654-3447

Nitro-Pak Preparedness Center, Inc.
www.nitro-pak.com
151 North Main St.
Heber City, UT 84032
800-866-4876

www.longlifefoods.com

Ready Reserve Foods, Inc.
www.readyreservefoods.com
1442 S. Gage St.
San Bernadino, CA 92408
800-453-2202

Grain Master Whisper Mill:
www.pleasanthillgrain.com
1604 N. Hwy. 14
Aurora, NE 68818
800-321-1073

Hand Operated Grain Mills;
Country Living Products
www.countrylivinggrainmills.com
14727 56th Ave. NW
Stanwood, WA 98292
360-652-0671

Wheat and Grains:
Home Grown Harvest
www.homegrownharvest.com
2065 Lakeshore Overlook Dr.
Kennesaw, GA 30152
866-900-3321

Successful cold storage

By Syliva Gist

Crisp carrot sticks, fresh cabbage, and fried potatoes from my Montana garden in June? Yes, but only if I've kept them in cold storage from last summer's garden.

A garden is a wise investment and provides the freshest, most nutritious vegetables available during the summer. But I need it to supply vegetables year-round, and that can be a challenge here in northwest Montana. I lean toward self-sufficiency and eating a local, seasonal, sustainable diet; we try to grow what we eat and eat what we grow. We preserve, dehydrate, and freeze both fruits and vegetables, making a trip to the fruit room or freezer a real delight throughout the winter. But I also like to eat some fresh veggies and have succeeded in storing carrots, potatoes, cabbage, and onions until just about the time the next crop is ready. I manage to keep beets, pumpkins, squash, and apples into late winter.

Ideally, I would have a root cellar which maintained the correct temperature for the produce I would like to keep. Unfortunately, it's not that ideal, so I have to look for other places to store things. Fortunately, different vegetables like different temperatures, so everything doesn't have to go in the same place. Other storage options (depending upon the item) include in the ground, under a staircase, unheated rooms, outside stairwells, pits in the ground, or extra refrigerators, to name a few.

A storage method is only the last step to having successful cold storage and fresh vegetables in the winter. The first step begins with the seed catalog; it is extremely important to choose cultivars which store well. For example, not every type of carrot will still be edible the following May. Most seed catalogs are good at telling us which ones have good storage qualities. I have relied on their recommendations and have found particular cultivars of a number of vegetables that store very well for me.

Planting time and harvest time also affect the success of storage. Many storage vegetables are planted later and harvested after frost. In the following discussion, I will note what works best for me as I deal with a fairly short growing season and cool nights.

Carrots

The carrot named **Bolero**, a nantes-type hybrid, is a dual purpose carrot. It can be planted early for delicious sweet carrots, but when planted later (in June here), it will achieve a nice size of 6 to 7 inches in length with a 1-1½ inch diameter in time for fall storage. After storage, this carrot will still be crisp and sweet. Harvest as late as possible, after frost, but before the ground freezes. I snap off the green tops right where they join the carrot.

I choose nice straight healthy carrots of good size for storage and bag up the forked, broken, nicked, small, or oversized ones to put in the refrigerator for immediate use in canning, juicing, or munching. Then I take five-gallon plastic buckets, clean washed sand, and a pitcher of water to dampen it. Don't put too much water in the sand as it will pool in the bottom and make it too soggy. I try to dampen the sand in a different container and add the sand to my storage bucket as needed. First I put down a layer of sand and lay carrots side by side. I prefer the carrots don't touch. Then in goes another layer of sand to cover the first layer of carrots. I continue pressing carrots into the sand and adding sand until I am near the top of the bucket, where I put on an extra thick layer of sand and lay the lid on top.

This bucket is very heavy, so I put the carrots into it at the site it will spend the winter, which, for me, is at the bottom of a stairwell leading into the basement from the garage. When the weather gets really cold,

I throw some rugs and blankets over the buckets to keep them from freezing. For ideal storage, carrots prefer 32° to 40° F and 90 to 95% humidity. If you don't have varmints underground looking for a free meal in winter, you can store them in the ground with a thick layer of mulch to prevent freezing.

Potatoes

Potatoes are a traditional fresh storage food, but all cultivars are not equal. The challenge is to have an edible supply year around.

Last fall I stored Red Norland, Sangre Red, Yukon Gold, and Kennebec potatoes of all sizes. Red Norland sprouted first, followed by Kennebec, Yukon Gold, and Sangre Red. **Sangre Red**, also called Sangre, is a round-to-oblong, white fleshed red potato with shallow eyes. It is a very good new potato as well as being great for storage. Digging them is easy, as they generally cluster very near the plant; it is also a heavy producer. Even though a local nursery lists them as so-so keepers, Sangre has been the last to sprout in storage, with the largest potatoes keeping the best. I will eventually have to pull the sprouts from them also, but I do not have ideal storage facilities—just a room in the basement where I keep my canned goods, where the temperature ranges between 50° and 60° F during the year. Potatoes prefer 40 degrees. Colder temperatures will turn them sugary. Much too crisp and juicy for hash browns in the fall, these Sangres reach the perfect condition for frying in June and July.

By planting these early season potatoes the end of May, I get large potatoes by the end of August, which I harvest in late September. Planting earlier, I can have new potatoes earlier, but for storage it works better to plant later here where frosts may kill the tops the first of June and potatoes grow well into summer as the nights are cool and the days moderate.

Cabbage

One of the greatest challenges in storing vegetables has been the cabbage. I tried a number of methods, but nothing worked until I started to grow cabbage especially bred for storage. So far my favorite is **Storage #4** (available from Johnny's Seeds). It will produce a large, very solid head, which is still nice and solid the following June.

While I start my early cabbages in March (eight weeks before the last expected spring frost), I start the storage cabbages the first week in May, about 100 to 120 days before the first expected frost in the fall, as it will make most of its head late in summer, but grow some and hold well into fall. I dig mine before the ground freezes or before the weather stays below freezing. I cut off the root, leaving 6 inches of the stalk, and trim off those loose outer leaves. I then wrap each very loosely in a plastic grocery bag and store them in the extra refrigerator or upside down in the stairwell next to the buckets I store the carrots in. During the cold months, they do best in the stairwell where ventilation is better. They prefer 32-40 degrees with 90% humidity. As the temperature rises outside, I have to move them to a refrigerator to last into summer. They can produce cabbagey fumes, which may make one reconsider keeping them in the house long term.

Onions

Perhaps my favorite vegetable in storage is the onion. The sweet ones have to be eaten in the summer and early fall, but the pungent ones can last until you have the next crop. A couple of long-day hybrids, **Copra** and **Norstar**, have worked well for me. I start the seed indoors in February, feed them fish fertilizer, and set tiny plants out in early May. Norstar matures sooner than Copra, but both are narrow necked hard onions of medium size. In August, I quit watering them.

When they mature, pull and dry them in the sun. If the weather isn't warm enough, it is necessary to push the tops over and then pull them and lay them out to dry for quite a while. When they have dried sufficiently, remove the dry tops (but not the skins) and put the onions in a basket or mesh bag and set or hang in a dry, cold (32° to 35° F) place where they get ventilation. I don't have a perfect place, but these two cultivars do well even when ideal storage can't quite be met.

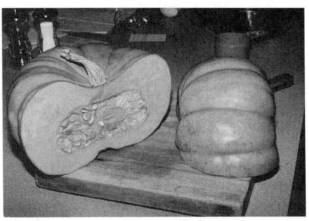

Heirloom Australian blue squash in mid-winter

For those who prefer non-hybrids, the yellow potato onion, a multiplier onion, is terrific. They are smaller (up to 1½ inch), but store extremely well, being very hard well into summer. You plant this onion in early fall and mulch for winter. Remove the mulch in spring to find sprouts which can soon provide green scallions or grow (with liberal watering) into bunches of small onions which will dry down in July. Be sure to save some to plant for the next crop.

Squash and pumpkins

An easy crop to store is squash or pumpkins. Nearly all kinds labeled winter squash and even mature summer squash, such as the **Mideast Cousa** type, can keep almost six months if they are picked at the right time and cured properly. At harvest, the skin should be so hard that a fingernail won't puncture it. Leave the stem on and cure both squash and pumpkin in the sun at 70° to 80° F for 10 to 14 days. If properly cured and later stored at 55° to 60° F with 60 to 70% humidity, they should hold through most of the winter. An unheated bedroom works well for me. Pies from fresh pumpkin taste delicious in March.

Beets

I hadn't even considered storing beets until a few that I had just thrown in a plastic bag in the refrigerator were in pretty good shape a couple of months later. Upon investigation, I discovered that, although the common Detroit Dark Red that I was planting can be stored if done properly, there are specific beets for winter storage. I purchased some **Lutz Greenleaf** seed and sowed it in the spring along with my other spring beets. It took a long time to germinate and then grew slowly, but in October, I dug some softball sized beets to store. Unless you are using a long season beet like Lutz, the seed should be sown in June or July for late harvest.

Beets tend to be more susceptible to frost damage (their shoulders often stick out of the ground), so they should be harvested before a killing frost. Harvest only mature beets and cut off the tops, leaving an inch of stem. Do not remove any of the root tip. Brush off the dirt and pack in layers in damp sawdust, sand, or moss. Keep cold (near 32° F) and very moist at 90 to 85% humidity. As mentioned before, unwashed beets keep quite a while in bags in a refrigerator. Depending upon storage conditions, beets can last anywhere from two to five months in storage.

Winter radishes

If you like radishes, you can enjoy them throughout the winter if you plant the winter type. There are a number of cultivars which lend themselves to storage: **Miyashige** (fall harvest Daikon), **Long Black Spanish, Misato Rose Flesh, China Rose, Round Black Spanish,** and **Radish Sakwiajima Mammoth,** to name a few. Generally, the planting date is July or early August, but each cultivar could be different, so pay attention to what the seed catalog tells you and adjust for your particular growing season. These radishes use more space; they not only may grow larger roots, but their tops are more leafy. Harvest in the fall and store only perfect roots. Trim off the leafy tops and treat like carrots, layered in moist sand, moss, or sawdust in your coldest above freezing storage place. They should last until February if stored properly.

Rutabagas/turnips

Rutabagas, known also as Swede turnips, are good candidates for storage. The turnip, however, gets mixed reviews. Johnny's Seeds doesn't recommend turnip storage, but some people have done it. Plant **Purple Top White Globe** in July or August and harvest three-inch maximum roots before heavy frost, cut off the tops, and treat them like carrots.

Laurentian and **Purple Top** (rutabaga, not turnip) are two common rutabaga cultivars recommended for winter storage. Plant in mid-June to mid-July or 90 days before intended harvest. Wait until there has been at least a couple of good frosts, usually October here, before digging for storage. If the roots are working their way out of the ground, I would hill some soil over them or mulch them when there may be a chance of freezing so the roots don't get damaged before I harvest. Cut off the tops and store like carrots. However, rutabagas shrivel easier than carrots, so you want to be sure to keep them moist. They can be waxed (sometimes you see them waxed in the supermarkets) to reduce dehydration; beeswax would be best if you choose this route. Rutabagas can be expected to last for two to four months in storage.

Celeriac

Celeriac, sometimes described as turnip-rooted celery, is an excellent keeper. **Monarch** and **Brilliant** are two good cultivars available. The trick with celeriac is the planting time. Start indoors (slow to germinate) in April but do not set out in the garden until June when the temperatures are averaging above 50° F. If the weather is too cold, the plant will think that it has passed through the first summer (in your house or greenhouse) and is in the winter cool down; when it warms up, the plant may bolt and go to seed.

Celeriac requires rich soil and plenty of moisture like celery, but is actually easier to grow. You don't want the plant to mature too early and get woody before you harvest. When you dig celeriac, break off the stocks, brush off the dirt, and remove long fine roots, if desired. It will keep a while on a shelf in the cellar; for the long haul, layer in moist sand, moss, or sawdust. Keep at 32° to 40° F with 90 to 95% humidity.

Parsnips

Rated as the hardiest of all root vegetables, the parsnip could be awarded "best of show" when it comes to storage. **Harris Model** and related cultivars are popular. Since all parsnips are intended for storage, choose one that fits your needs (some are resistant to disease, etc.). Dig a deep bed and plant fresh seeds early in the spring, March through May (depending upon your season). Be patient as they may germinate slowly (up to 28 days). It takes a long season (100-120 days) and freezing weather to produce tasty parsnips. Frosty weather helps starch in the root turn to sugar so they taste sweeter. Then you can begin harvest.

You actually have four options. You can take advantage of all four. First, after a few moderate to heavy frosts, you can dig some to eat immediately. Because the roots can get very long, digging, not pulling, is recommended. Or to keep the ground from freezing, put down some mulch so you can dig later.

Even though the ground may not freeze under the mulch, you may not want to go out and dig in mid-winter; dig and store some in the cellar. These roots should have the leaves trimmed and be stored like carrots in damp sand, moss, or sawdust. Ideal conditions are 32-35 degrees and 90-95% humidity.

And for the final option, when the ground thaws in the spring, go out and dig the sweetest parsnips. They will be good until new leaves are formed; they get woody after they begin to grow. With parsnips, the last really could be the best.

Apples

Apples are the only fruit I have tried to store fresh through the winter. Since there are hundreds of cultivars, there should be quite a few that store well. The nursery catalogs will usually indicate that attribute. Usually, the storage apple will ripen late, so that it can be picked in cool weather. The apple I have had great success with is **Honeycrisp**. It has a sweet-tart flavor and is exceptionally crisp, features that were still noticeable after months in my extra refrigerator. Although a tad shriveled, they made excellent applesauce.

Some helpful pointers in harvesting apples: pick mature fruit, leave the stem on the apple, and cool fruit overnight before storing if the day is somewhat warm. Apples last best if stored near 32° F at 80 to 90% humidity; the warmer the temperatures, the faster they soften. They should be kept in shallow layers in baskets or slatted crates; they also need to be checked for spoilage occasionally. It is wonderful to have some homegrown fresh fruit to go with all those winter vegetables. They should be stored separately, though, as apples give off ethylene gas, which ages vegetables.

General harvesting tips

In cold storage, we are taking advantage of the plant's natural dormant stage between seasons. Success rates are also raised by following proven guidelines. Harvesting in dry, cool weather is helpful because cold weather encourages the vegetables to store sugars and starches rather than water in the roots. Brush off the dirt gently, but cleaning isn't necessary. Don't bruise the produce. Store only the best produce; bruised, broken, or nicked vegetables should be used soon. Tops should be clipped immediately; if left on, they suck moisture from the root. Many tops are good to eat; chop some and dehydrate to add to soups later.

Folklore recommends that you pick apples and harvest root vegetables during the decrease of the moon, in the third and fourth quarters, because bruised spots will dry, not rot, and the food will keep better. If you follow the moon in planting and harvesting, you might want to keep this in mind also.

Two books which have been helpful for me to pursue my goal of providing the kitchen with year around vegetables from my garden are *Root Cellaring* by Mike and Nancy Bubel and *Four-Season Harvest* by Eliot Coleman. The first is about the natural cold storage of fruits and vegetables, with drawings for possible root cellars (and alternate hideaways) and details of how to store many different varieties of garden produce. Coleman's book is basically about ways to extend your gardening season, but includes a chapter on root cellars and indoor harvesting. Reading these books opened my eyes to the possibilities of having a larger variety of fresh vegetables from my own garden throughout the year.

Successful cold storage review

1. Select the best cultivar.
2. Plant at the right time.
3. Harvest at the right time.
4. Store properly.

I follow these steps, keep notes on planting and harvesting dates to determine the right time for my area, and store under the best conditions I have available. It can work for you too. 🐾

Canning

"*If more of us valued food and cheer and song
above hoarded gold, it would be a merrier world.*"

J.R.R. Tolkien

Canning basics

By Jackie Clay

Like everyone else, sometimes I forget that homesteading chores I have done for years can be a complete mystery to those new to homesteading. Home canning is certainly one of these, as BHM writer, Jeff Yago, brought up to me recently.

So Jeff, and all you other less experienced home canners, let's take a look at the basics of home canning starting with the two most common methods of home canning.

Boiling water bath canning

Most folks first begin canning using the boiling water bath method of canning, which is also known as the hot water bath. "Bad" bacteria, such as *salmonella*, *staphylococcus aureus* (staph), and *clostridium botulinum* (which causes botulism, a type of food poisoning) thrive only in low acid foods such as meats, poultry, and vegetables, and require special precautions I'll discuss later. However, canning high acid foods such as pickles, fruits (including acidic tomatoes), jams, preserves, and jellies can be done with a simple boiling water bath.

Most people are familiar with using the big dark blue kettle with tiny white flakes and the handy wire rack for holding and separating jars for boiling water bath canning, as this is usually the "standard" for this process. But I have also used a wide array of alternative "canners." One of these was my grandmother's copper boiler, which was a covered oval kettle, which was so big that it took two burners of the old gas stove in the basement to heat it. (In case you're wondering, the boiler was used in the "old" days to boil clothes on wash day.) I've also used kettles smaller than the big blue canner, such as soup pots, for small batches, like when I only had a couple of jars of jelly to put up on that day. Another "alternative" boiling water bath canner has been my large pressure canner, with the lid simply set on, not locked down or under pressure. In a pinch, I've also used steel buckets with a board for a lid.

The only thing really needed to water bath can is a container that you can sit on the stove that is deep enough to let the boiling water cover the jars by at least one inch and contain the water at a rolling boil for the time it takes to process the jars of food.

One vital tip: You *must* use either the wire rack that comes with the canning kettle or rig up something else to keep the canning jars off the bottom of the kettle while they are processing. If this is not done, the jars will usually have their bottoms broken out. I bought a couple of different sized barbecue grill grates at the dollar store, sized to fit two of my smaller stew pots for times I am running a small batch. You can also fold a kitchen towel and lay it flat under the jars. (No, it will not scorch.)

It is necessary that you have a lid for your container when you water bath can for you to get the pot up to a good rolling boil as rapidly as possible while processing jars of food. Otherwise, the food gets simmered much too long and can become soft or discolored. (Who wants soggy pickles or dark peach preserves?) This lid does not have to be a special lid, although using the lid that came with the pot ensures a good fit.

With the boiling water bath method of canning, you fill hot, clean jars with hot food, usually to within half an inch of the top. After carefully wiping the rim of the jar clean with a clean, damp cloth, you place a hot, previously boiled lid on the jar, then screw down a ring firmly tight. Using a jar lifter, the filled jars are placed into simmering hot water in the water bath canner, making sure that the water covers all the jars by at least one inch. The top is placed on and the heat is turned back on. The processing time *begins* when the water in the kettle reaches a good rolling boil. After the processing time is up, turn off the heat and carefully lift the pot lid open, away from you to avoid scalding from the billowing steam. Then lift the jars out carefully using the jar lifter to avoid burning your hands, and place them to cool on a dry, folded towel. Keep the jars out of drafts (open windows, fans, or opening doors) while they cool.

Resist the temptation to wipe residue off the jar lids or poke at them to "get them to seal." These may, in fact, interfere with the jar lids sealing. Also, never tighten the rings further at this point. Instructions in canning books or manuals that read "complete seal, if necessary" do not apply to modern two-piece canning lids and rings. Leave the jars alone until they are cool, often overnight. Then you may take off the rings and wash the jars in mild warm soapy water in the kitchen sink to clean up any "stickies" before you put them in the pantry to store. Taking off the rings does *not* jeopardize the keeping power of the jar; it is either sealed or not. In fact, keeping the rings on the jars may cause rusting under the rings due to condensation, especially if the jars are stored in a basement.

Sterilizing jars

When water bath canning, be especially watchful for directions in the recipe you are using for instructions to place the food to be canned in hot sterilized jars. This is most often seen in preserves or pickles that have little or no water bath processing time. *If you don't sterilize the jars, your food is open to mold or unwanted fermentation.*

Do you need special equipment for this sterilization? No. Simply boil your clean, empty jars in your water bath canner and simmer them for 10 minutes or so. Then hold in the hot water until you are ready to use them. This keeps them not only sterile, but also hot, which is usually required. (If it is not, remove the jars, draining the water out of them well, and place them on a clean folded towel to dry and await filling.)

If sterilizing the jars is not mentioned, the jars only need to be as clean as any other glass you would use to drink out of.

Canning peaches with your water bath canner

Okay, let's can peaches to see how to use the water bath canner. The basic process is the same, but there are differences for each food, so read your canning manual before starting.

1. Get out your jars, and check for cracks or nicks in the rim; any damaged jars need to be thrown away because they will not seal and will often break during processing.

2. Wash jars and rings in hot soapy water. Rinse and leave in hot water until needed.

3. Select only sound, ripe peaches (unripe peaches will not peel easily).

4. To peel peaches, dip them in a kettle of boiling water for a minute only, then drain and put into cold water. This loosens the skin, making them easy to slip off.

5. Cut peaches in half. Remove pit. Leave in halves or cut into desired slices. Drop pieces into a large bowl containing cold water and either half a cup of lemon juice or a commercial product to prevent darkening, such as Fruit Fresh.

6. Place jar on dry folded towel and pack peaches, leaving half an inch of head space (head space is just room at the top of the jar).

7. Pick out enough new jar lids for your jars and bring to a boil in enough water to just cover them. Keep them in hot water until you are ready to use them.

8. Cover peaches with boiling hot syrup (see your manual for proportions of this sugar and water solution), leaving half an inch of head space.

9. Slide a wooden spoon or rubber spatula down between the peaches to let air bubbles escape and more syrup contact the fruit.

10. Wipe the jar rim well with a clean damp cloth. Place hot lid on jar and screw down ring firmly tight. Use no force.

11. Place jars on rack of full, hot, water bath canner. Never place hot jars in contact with anything cold or vice versa, as they will break.

12. When the canner is full, the water should cover all of the jars by one inch. If you need to add more water, use a tea kettle of hot water to bring the level up to the necessary point.

13. Bring water to a rolling boil with the top on the canner. When it begins to boil vigorously, begin your timing. For altitudes below 1,000 feet, you'll need to process your peaches for 25 minutes for pints and 30 minutes for quarts.

14. When the time is up, turn off heat and remove the jars from the canner carefully with a jar lifter. Place on a dry folded towel, out of drafts, to cool. Don't tighten any bands that seem loose. The jars will seal. When the jars are cool (overnight), inspect seals. A sealed jar will have a tight indentation in the center of the flat lid. It will not give on pressure from a finger in the center. The contents of an unsealed jar should be eaten at once or refrigerated.

15. Remove the bands and wash if necessary. The bands are not necessary to maintain the seal and may cause rust to form. Store the jars in a dark, dry, relatively cool place.

That's all there is to water bath canning. If you can boil water and tell time, you can do it easily.

Pressure canning

While the molds, enzymes, and yeasts that could spoil your home-canned food are quite easily killed by the relatively lower temperatures seen in processing in a boiling water bath, the dangerous bacteria, especially *clostridium botulinum*, which causes the potentially deadly botulism food poisoning, require a much higher temperature to destroy. Because of bacterial spores, all low acid food, such as vegetables and meats, must be processed at a *much* higher temperature than is possible by simply boiling in a hot water bath canner, no matter how long the jars are boiled. The food must be brought to 240° F, and this is done by using a pressure canner. In the pressure canner, the lid is sealed tightly and the contents are heated under pressure for the necessary processing time for each food canned.

In the old days folks didn't have a pressure canner available, so they boiled low acid foods, such as sweet corn or green beans, for hours on end. This was, and still is, an *extremely dangerous* practice, as no matter how long you boil food you can not kill the spores that give off toxins which cause botulism. This is where all those stories about people getting sick, even dying, after eating home-canned foods come from.

The only safe method of processing low acid foods, such as vegetables, meats, poultry, or any recipe containing these foods (soups, stews, etc.) is by pressure canning.

Types of pressure canners

Pressure canners are basically large, heavy duty aluminum or stainless steel pots with heavy lids which may be tightly fastened, either by twisting the lid down into notches or by black bakelite knobs that are screwed down to hold the lid in place. Some canners employ both methods.

There are two types of pressure canners: those with a dial and those with weights. I much prefer the canners with a gauge, providing the gauge is checked periodically for accuracy. This is easily done through your County Extension Office for little or no cost to you. You need to know that your gauge is accurate to prevent underprocessing your food. With an accurate gauge, you can immediately see what is happening and whether your pressure is rising, necessitating turning down the heat a little.

But lacking a canner with a gauge, you can certainly use one with a weighted gauge.

Don't bother with a "pressure cooker/canner" saucepan. These are too small for serious canners and are priced just a little below a "real" canner.

Also, some canners come with a rubber gasket ring, which seals the lid to the body of the canner. Others, which are a little more expensive when bought new, have a beveled "metal-to-metal" fitting that does not require a rubber gasket. The rubber gasket will last several years, depending on usage each year, then it will begin to get stiff and crack, resulting in steam loss and poor processing and uneven pressure. Before you see these results, you should replace the gasket that is getting stiff.

For this reason, I prefer the steel to steel sealing, without a gasket.

As with the water bath canner, you need some sort of a rack between your jars and the bottom of the canner to prevent overheating and breaking the jars' bottoms out. This rack can be a separate liner kettle, as I have in my huge canner. Or it can be a simple wire rack to allow the water to circulate under the jars.

Cautions when pressure canning

Everyone has heard the old tales of pressure canners blowing up in the kitchen. I think this is the single most common reason people are afraid to pressure can. Yes, this could happen, but the chances of it happening when a person uses care and follows the directions in their canning manual are minute. I've been pressure canning for over 35 years and have never blown up a canner. Nor has my mother before me.

Before each canning session, run a string through your exhaust vents to ensure they are not plugged by corrosion or bits of food. Follow your canner's direction manual. Likewise, follow a good, up-to-date canning manual or book each and every time you can food.

Don't try to do too many things at once. When you pressure can, you *must* stay in the kitchen and keep a careful eye on the pressure. Don't wash clothes, answer the phone, play with the kids, or read a novel while you can. Pressures can climb very quickly at times. And it is possible that a safety could malfunction. Usually a safety valve will blow steam at just a little above 16 pounds or so. But it is always possible that the valve could malfunction at a critical time. Better to keep watch.

General pressure canning goes something like this (but remember to follow your directions each time you can):

- The food is cut and packed into clean jars, according to directions.
- The rim of the jar is wiped clean with a clean, damp cloth.
- A previously boiled, hot lid is placed on the jar and the ring is screwed down firmly tight.
- The jars are placed in the canner on the rack.
- There is usually about two inches of warm water in the canner, which produces the steam to pressure can (again, follow your canner's directions).
- The pressure canner lid is placed on and twisted into place and/or the knobs tightened. When tightening knobs, set the lid down evenly, then begin tightening two knobs on alternate sides at the same time. When these two are tight, again grasp two alternate knobs and tighten them at the same time, repeating until all are very snug. This method seals the top down nice and even, preventing steam leaks.

• With the relief valves open, turn on the heat. You must exhaust steam powerfully on pressure canners. This ensures that when the valve is closed off to build pressure that the correct heat is produced. Follow your canner's manual regarding this; some say to exhaust steam for x number of minutes, where others say to close the petcock when steam is exhausting "forcefully." This means really hissing loudly and steadily out of the valve, not just alternate fits of "sisses."

• When the steam has exhausted adequately, close off the petcocks or set the weight in place. But don't begin counting until your pressure has reached the pressure you will need to process the food.

• Keep the pressure even during the entire processing time by raising or lowering the heat under the canner, as needed, in small adjustments. When canning on a woodstove, you sometimes have to slide the canner off the hottest spot to do this, then back after the fire dies down a little. This is quite a dance, but I've canned an awful lot of food on my wood kitchen range. With experience, you learn to adjust your fire with the types and thicknesses of wood you are burning, as well as using the oven draft to regulate the heat. It also helps to open the oven door at times, which reduces the stovetop heat. You learn pretty fast when doing it.

• After being certain that the pressure in your canner has remained at or, perhaps at times, slightly above the recommended pressure for the processing time indicated in your canning manual, turn off the heat. If you are canning on a wood range, very carefully remove the entire canner from the heat. I just slide mine to the right, off the heating surface and onto the warming wing of the stove, which remains relatively cool during canning—cool enough that the pressure quickly begins to fall. If your stove is minus this wing, you'll have to carefully lift the canner onto a table or the kitchen counter. Don't clunk the jars together.

- Wait until the pressure returns to zero. Do not be tempted to hurry the process by tinkering with the weight or the exhaust valve. This will only result in jars that do not seal properly. I know because when I was canning a truckload of sweet corn, I faced just such a temptation at 3 a.m. and my groggy mind prompted me to just let "a little" steam escape at a time. The result was 9 quarts and 16 pints of sweet corn that did not seal. (Oh they seemed to, at first, until after a couple of days on my pantry shelves. Then the seals all failed, and all 15 jars of sweet corn had to be dumped out and buried in the garden. A very hard lesson.)

- After the pressure has returned to zero, open the petcocks and/or steam valves and let all remaining steam escape. Then take the lid off the canner, directing any steam away from your face and arms.

- Using a jar lifter, carefully take each jar out and place it on a dry, folded towel, out of drafts. Allow adequate air space between jars. I've found that this helps them to seal quickly and effectively. Never leave jars in the canner because you can't wait around for the pressure to return to zero. Again, during my sweet corn frenzy...yep, I screwed up again. And again, I lost the whole batch due to my own lazy thinking. Or was it being brain-dead at 4 a.m?

- As the jars cool, you'll hear satisfying "pings" from the lids as they are drawn down in the center, creating a perfect seal. Don't poke at, or otherwise handle, the lids while they are still warm. When they are cooled, you can gently touch the center of each lid. When it is firm and indented in the center, the seal is complete. If there is *any* give at all or the center is not indented, the seal is not complete, and this food must either be refrigerated and eaten quite soon or totally reprocessed with another batch right away. Do not let an unsealed jar sit out on the counter for any length of time, as it is possible for it to begin to spoil.

• Once the jars have cooled, again, overnight, you should remove the rings and wash the jars in warm soapy water, if necessary. Don't worry, you won't make the seal release by this gentle process. You'll only make the jars store nicer, as the rings won't rust and the sides will remain glistening clean. Such residue as corn juice can cause dirt to stick to the jars, making a less-than-beautiful jar.

Making chili using a pressure canner

Let's do up a batch of chili. Most foods are pressure canned in nearly the same way, but, again, check your canning manual for other foods. For recipes with mixed ingredients, simply process the food for the longest length of time required for any single ingredient. In this case, it's meat.

1. Select crack and nick-free jars.

2. Make a large pot of your favorite chili; the beans do not have to be completely tender, but well cooked.

3. Wash jars in hot soapy water, then rinse, keeping hot until needed.

4. Boil enough lids for your jars and keep in hot water until needed.

5. Place jar on dry folded towel and carefully ladle your chili into the jar, leaving one inch head space.

6. Wipe jar rim with damp, clean cloth. Place hot lid on and screw down ring firmly tight. Use no force.

7. Place jars on rack in pressure canner, containing two inches of hot water. (Or the amount recommended by manufacturer.)

8. Fasten pressure canner lid firmly with steam valves open. Turn on heat.

9. Exhaust steam forcefully for 10 minutes.

10. Close petcock or vent, allowing pressure to build.

11. Hold at correct pressure (10 pounds for altitudes below 1,000 feet) for an hour and fifteen minutes (pints), or an hour and a half (quarts). Adjust heat as needed.

12. When time is up, turn off heat. When gauge returns to zero, carefully release any remaining steam and remove lid, taking care to avoid any steam in canner.

13. Lift out jars carefully with jar lifter and place on a dry, folded towel, away from drafts, to cool. Do not tighten any loose bands.

14. When cool, check for seal. Sealed jars dent inward and do not give under the pressure of a finger in the center.

15. Remove rings and wash jars. Store in a dark, cool, dry place.

I told you it was easy.

When opening the jar, again check the seal, then open it and inspect and sniff the product. If any of these raises questions of quality, throw it out where animals and children can not get hold of it. To be safe, always bring low-acid foods to boiling temperature for 15 minutes before eating.

Now, using your home food processing skills, you can effectively and cheaply stock up enough food to last your family through any hard time. Be sure to store goodies, such as fruits, favorite canned recipes, jams, pickles, etc. When one is having worries, nothing helps like a little treat.

Other canning equipment

Canning book or manual. No home canning should be attempted without a relatively current canning book or manual on hand, no matter how much you may have canned. You just can't trust your memory that much. Each and every time I prepare to can a batch of food, I *always* get out my canning book and check and recheck the directions on that particular food. Everyone should make this their practice too.

I say "relatively current," as there have been some changes in canning methods over the years. Generally, the times have increased by about five minutes, probably to keep us safer. And there are a few other changes to go with the times. For instance, so many folks are growing "low-acid" tomatoes that it is best to add lemon juice or vinegar to tomatoes that are home-canned. This was not the practice 10 years ago. So, the bottom line is: Get a recent canning book or manual for up-to-date instructions.

Canning jars. Canning jars come in several sizes from tiny 4-oz. jars for "gourmet" specialties, usually meant as gifts, up through half pint, pint, quart, and half-gallon. Some older jars are even quart and a half. And among these jars there are both "regular" openings and "wide-mouth." Within this vast array, there are definite uses for all of them. While lids for wide-mouthed jars cost more than do regular-sized lids, it is much easier to fill and retrieve food from a wide-mouthed jar than the narrower regular opening. Such things as chunks of roast, large dill pickles, cheese, and poultry with the bone left in slide quite easily out of the wide-mouthed jar, where you sometimes have to really dig to retrieve these foods from a narrow-mouthed jar.

But, because the regular lids are considerably cheaper (neither is costly), I do the bulk of my canning in regular jars of all sizes.

I totally disagree with my *Ball Blue Book* canning manual (so sorry, guys), in that I have been using "alternative" canning jars for thirty-some years, and have never found them "weaker" or less desirable than regular Mason jars. My only requirements for canning jars are that canning lids and rings fit correctly on the jar and that they are free of cracks or nicks, just like my Mason jars. Don't attempt to use plastic screw-on lids, etc., that come with these alternative jars, for canning. You need the two-piece lids to assure satisfactory sealing. Some of my alternative jars have previously housed salad dressing, mayonnaise, peanut butter, and my mom's Sanka. And I can year after year after year in them, including pressure canning corn, beans, and meats. No worries.

Rings and lids. The modern two-piece vacuum lids and rings are the only way to go. Yes, you probably can process some foods, such as pickles and fruits, in the old zinc tops with rubber rings, but it is much safer and easier to use the two-piece lids. Cheaper, too, as the rings (which are only useable once) are quite a bit more expensive than the flat tops used in modern canning. This is one instance where I feel that the old ways are not the best way to go.

You can reuse the rings year after year, as long as they are sound and screw down firmly. But the round, flat lids should only be used once, then discarded.

Canning funnel. A canning funnel is a "must" for quick, easy filling of your jars. You can either buy a plastic or aluminum funnel, usually for less than $2. My current funnel is about 20-years-old. They last a long, long time, providing that you don't lose it. (My last one ran away to one of the kid's sand piles and was never heard from again.) Not only does the funnel hurry up canning, but it keeps the rim of the jars cleaner during filling than when you just ladle the food in without it.

Jar lifter. I would hate to try to can without a jar lifter, although I'll admit that I made it a season without one. This simple tool allows you to firmly grasp and lift scalding hot jars. Without one, you'll burn your fingers and break jars. I'll guarantee it. The cost is less than $5 and, again, mine is over 20-years-old. The kids don't seem to find this as fascinating as the funnel.

Other handy tools to have on hand are a non-metallic spatula or other tool to run down along the sides of filled jars to release air bubbles (I use a single chopstick—works for me), tongs, saucepans for heating lids, good sharp knives, mixing bowls, soup pots for recipes, and a clock or timer to be sure you process your food correctly.

Head space

All canning instructions tell us to leave "X" amount of room as "head space." This means that 1 inch, ½ inch, or whatever space is left unfilled at the top of our canning jars. Some foods swell and need a bit more room, so they do not touch the lid. Others do not and, thus, do not require much headroom at all. If you do not allow enough head space, food may boil out of the jar and residue may prevent the jar from sealing. But if you leave too much head space, there might not be sufficient processing to drive all the air out of the jar and the food may spoil. You don't need a tape measure every time you can, but you should make a conscious effort to follow the head space directions quite closely.

Hot pack and raw pack

All food that is packed into jars is either hot (hot packed) or raw (raw packed) when you pack it into jars. Different recipes require different packing methods. Cold or raw pack is often used for time-saving canning, where hot packing allows more food to be packed into jars, and thus requires fewer jars to put up the same amount of food. The term "cold pack" is sometimes used by some people to denote boiling water bath canning. This is an incorrect interpretation of the word and can be confusing to beginners. Follow your canning manual and recipe as to which method you should use. If the recipe gives both, use whichever you feel comfortable with. The end result will be nearly the same.

One note here: fruits and tomatoes that are raw packed will float to the top of the jar leaving a couple of inches of juice below them. This makes some beginners think they have made some sort of error in their canning. Not to worry. This is natural, given the method of canning. You wouldn't want to show these jars of fruit at the county fair, but they will eat just as well as their hot-packed cousins.

Altitude charts

The processing times for boiling water bath canning and the amount of pressure called for in pressure canning are for foods which are canned at altitudes of 1,000 feet above sea level or less. If you live where the altitude is higher, you must adjust the processing time when processing food in a boiling water bath canner and the amount of pressure when processing food in a pressure canner according to the altitude figure in the altitude chart shown on the next page.

Storing your home-canned foods

When your jars have been checked to assure that they are, indeed, properly sealed (all lids are firmly indented and without give), washed and dried, they are ready to store. The very best place to store your home-canned food is in a cool, dry, dark area. A dry basement is ideal, but a cool, windowless pantry will also work well. You don't want to store food in a damp basement or root cellar because in as little as six months, any jars with rings will begin to rust under the ring, and in a year, even those without rings will show rust on the lids. After a while longer the rust will progress so much that it will completely eat though the lids, and the food will spoil.

Canned food should not be stored in a place that can freeze. If the food has frozen, it will still be edible unless the seal has been forced by expanding food. But frozen, then thawed canned food will tend to be soft and unappetizing. There's "edible" and then there's "good." Edible is not good enough for me.

A frequently asked question about canned food is "How long will it be good to eat?" Luckily, home-canned food is good almost indefinitely. I'm sure that after a few years there is some loss of nutrients, but that can be offset by serving it in combination with fresh food from the field or garden. The taste of

Altitude chart

Boiling water bath canner

Altitude (Feet)	Increase processing time
1,001-3,000	5 Minutes
3,001-6,000	10 Minutes
6,001 -8,000	15 Minutes
8,001-10,000	20 Minutes

Pressure canner

Altitude (Feet)	Dial gauge (PSI)	Weighted gauge
0-1,000	11	10
1,001-2,000	11	15
2,001-4,000	12	15
4,001-6,000	13	15
6,001-8,000	14	15
8,001-10,000	15	15

long-stored food is still good. Some foods tend to soften some during long storage. Berries, peaches, potatoes, and peas are some of these. But they are still definitely useable. I use softer berries and other fruits in yogurts, ice cream, desserts, puddings, etc. Softer vegetables go into soups and casseroles.

To avoid foods becoming too old and becoming soft or losing unnecessary nutrients, it's best to jot down the year of processing on the lid with a permanent marker. Then you can rotate your canned goods, using the oldest first, keeping the pantry full of the most current canning.

Opening your jars of home-canned foods

When you decide to have a jar of your home-canned food for a meal, don't just pop it open and dump it into a pan. Take a few safety precautions. (Very few jars of home-canned food ever go bad, but it's best to check, just to be sure.) The first thing you need to do is to *look at* the jar, including the seal. Does the food look normal, and not cloudy or with black or dark areas at the top? If it looks good, then carefully check the seal. Is it still firmly indented in the center, without any give? If so, great. Now carefully pry off the lid, taking care not to chip the rim of the jar with your opener. Be careful in your choice of can openers, as some just don't do a good job opening canning jars. Sometimes a cheap beer bottle opener attachment on a pocket knife is better than a twenty dollar can opener. This is one reason I always keep a pocket knife in my pocket.

But 99 percent of the time or better, your food is fine. Just to be very, very sure, never taste meats, vegetables, or combinations of these, such as soups and stews, until they have been brought up to boiling temperature for at least 15 minutes. This may be boiling or baking as in a casserole. Again, any "off" smells indicate possible spoiled food and you need to take steps to dispose of the food safely.

Any time you are in doubt about a food being good, dump it out in a place where no animals or humans have access to it. Never feed bad canned food to your dog, the chickens, or pigs. I either take it out into the fenced garden and bury it or dump it on the fire in my wood kitchen range. But again, *very little* home-canned food needs tossing out. It's a very good, safe way to put up food.

Canning manuals and books

As I've said, perhaps your most valuable home canning tool is a good canning manual or book. I have several, and absolutely *never* can anything without getting one out and reading the section on the food I am about to put up. Don't trust your memory. Always check. And be sure your canning manual or book is relatively current. You don't need a new one every year or two. But don't use your grandmother's old Kerr book, either.

There are several good, fairly recent canning books out there and also several manuals. You can also go to your County Extension Office, often located in the County Courthouse, and receive current low cost or free canning booklets.

Most stores that carry canning supplies carry the low cost *Ball Blue Book*, under $6 at last check. Or you can contact Jarden Home Brands, 1-800-240-3340 and online at www. homecanning.com

Some good canning books include:

- *Keeping the Harvest* by Nancy Chioffi & Gretchen Mead
- *The Big Book of Preserving the Harvest* by Costenbader
- *The Canning, Freezing, Curing, & Smoking of Meat, Fish and Game* by Wilbur Eastman
- *Ball Complete Book of Home Preserving*

Canning meat safely

By Jackie Clay

Of all the foods I can every year, the most useful is the wide variety of meats. While we aren't huge meat eaters, these rows and rows of jars of all sizes form the base of many meals throughout the year. And in our hurry-scurry world, it's so convenient to have this pre-cooked, tender, and oh-so-tasty meat right on the shelves, ready to quickly whip up a meal that tastes like I spent hours preparing it.

At any one time, you'll find jars of venison, moose, and elk meat, chicken, turkey, beef, ground meat, pork, and fish on my shelves. Two of the best things is that this meat was cheap (hunted, home-raised, or on sale) and it's so fast and easy to can. I am able to ready over a dozen meals' worth of meat in less than an hour. This is about the same amount of time it takes to prep and cook raw meat, and I have so many extra, ready-to-heat meals on my shelves.

Sure, you can freeze meat, as most people today do. But when you need that meat, you must either take hours to defrost it or use a microwave. Your meat can get buried with other things so long that it can become freezer burned, which gives the meat a bad smell and taste. When your meat is canned, it is all lined up in order and you can choose big chunks, steaks, slices or dices at a glance.

Last of all, and perhaps most important is that in a power outage of a week or more, you will lose all of the meat in your freezer unless you can somehow either keep it cold or move it all to another freezer some-where outside of the outage area. I lost a big freezer full during an out-age. I did all the right things; I covered it with heavy quilts, didn't open it much, etc. But after several days, I was about to lose food, so I began canning on my wood range. I did save a lot of the most important food, but still had buckets that had to be carried to the dogs and pigs. It was a sad time to see all that good food that we had worked so hard to raise and put up, get tossed away. I swore "never again" and began canning and dehydrating all my food instead of freezing it.

As a bonus, your own home-canned meat contains nothing but what you put in with it: meat, water, and possibly salt and spices. After all, who can feel good about eating something you can't even pronounce? Then there are the "hidden" ingredients in that store-bought canned meat—hormones, antibiotics, genetically-altered feed, bacteria, and mystery ingredients from sloppily processed meat.

But, you've heard, meat is hard to home can. You must be an expert to even think of trying it. If you do, you might poison your family. In reality, meat is very easy to can safely. If you have a pressure canner and can read directions, you can definitely do it. David, my sixteen year old son, has been helping me can meat since he was ten.

Basic equipment for home canning meat

Because meat is a low-acid food, it must be processed in a pressure canner. This allows the meat to be heated at a temperature higher than boiling, which kills the dangerous bacteria that could cause food poisoning or illness. In a pressure canner, the steam causes the internal temperature to rise to 240° F, which is a safe temperature to process low acid food. A simple boiling water bath canner only heats the **food to boiling, which is 180° F**. This does not allow the food to reach a high enough temperature to kill possible bacteria, no matter how long you process the food.

Yes, in the "old days" people did can meat in a boiling water bath for 3 hours, but this was NEVER SAFE and people always risked food poisoning by doing this. **You must use a pressure canner to home can meat.**

Meat may be canned in quarts, pints, or half-pint jars. I usually do some in each size. In the past, I usually canned in quarts, but then I always had leftovers which needed to be refrigerated. Then I got smart and started canning in smaller jars. Now there is no waste, and I find that I actually turn to those smaller jars very often.

There has been a huge, ongoing debate for years and years about using "other" than Kerr and Mason jars for home canning. Some folks claim stridently that if you use jars that once held salsa or mayonnaise they'll crack and break under pressure. But I can tell you that is not true. I've used hundreds of jars that were previously used for mayo, salsa, pickles, and more, for canning meat and other foods that must be pressure canned and those jars work just fine. Just make sure that a standard two-piece canning jar lid and ring fit the jar snugly. A major mayonnaise manufacturer uses jars that look like canning jars and the ring screws down, but when you add the lid, the ring just goes round and round, never tightening. Watch out for this.

When canning meat, it's a good idea to have a jar lifter, which is an inexpensive heavy wire tong that grasps steaming hot jars and lets you lift them out of the canner when the processing time is done.

Safety in using the pressure canner

We've all heard the horror stories about a steam pressure canner "blowing up" in Aunt Mary's kitchen, putting a hole in her ceiling. What they don't tell you is that Aunt Mary screwed up badly. It's just about impossible to blow up a modern pressure canner, but there are a few tips that will keep the process safe.

First, do not let any small children play around the stove when the canner is processing. This is just common sense. Canners are heavy and hot. Small children are curious and could pull the canner off the stove or turn the flame up under the canner without you noticing it.

When you are canning, don't get distracted. You have to be right there to watch the canner during the processing time. Sometimes it only takes a very few minutes for the pressure to go from a nice ten pounds to a wild fifteen.

Even then, there is a safety on modern canners that lets off excess steam, if necessary, but don't depend on that. Sometimes it will ruin the seals on your jars, going from a high pressure to a sudden drop. You don't want to have all your work ruined.

If your canner has a dial gauge, make sure it is accurate. It's best to take it to your extension office to have it checked before each canning season, especially if the canner is not new.

Make sure the vent holes in the canner's lid are open. I blow through mine each time I go to use it, to make absolutely sure the openings are clear. Sometimes a small bit of food gets forced up into the openings, blocking them. This is dangerous and could cause extreme pressure to build up.

Read your canning manual each and every time you process a jar of meat. There are many variables, depending on the recipe and preparation of the meat. I've been canning since 1964, and every time I begin to process a food, I check my canning manual, just to be sure. No one is perfect and I don't want to make a mistake. Meat is too precious, and so is the health and safety of my family.

Getting started

Let's start with the very easiest meat to home can: stew meat. This can be beef or venison, including moose and elk meat. I put by more stewing meat than any other type of meat, besides ground. The reason for this is that I can use it for such a wide variety of recipes, from shredded meat for tamales and barbecue, to stews, chunky chili, and casseroles.

I like to cut my meat when it is slightly frozen. This makes it firm and it cuts easily and quickly. Warm meat or even chilled meat is harder to slice than meat that has some ice crystals in it.

To make stew meat, cut the meat across the grain, into one inch thick slices, as if you were making large steaks. You don't have to cut the bone, just cut around it. Remove as much fat, gristle, and white muscle covering as you can. You want your home canned meat to be prime eating, and if you leave too much fat on the meat, you run the risk of having some jars not seal because the fat gets between the lid and rim of the jar during processing. Slice the meat into strips, then cut it into cubes.

Put the meat into a large mixing bowl and the scraps into another.

When you have a large amount, get out your canning jars and line them up on a folded clean towel on the table. Make sure there are no cracks or nicks in the rims of the jars. Then get out a box or two of lids, so you make sure you have them ready. Also find your jar rings and jar lifter. Set the pressure canner on the stove and put two inches of water in it, then the basket or bottom grate, depending on the brand of canner you are using.

Now get out your largest frying pan and put a tablespoonful of cooking oil in it and turn up the heat to medium. Add your meat until you have enough to fill the pan so the cubes are about two high. The reason you need to brown and partially cook the meat is twofold; it shrinks it, while adding flavor, and it heats the meat, getting it ready to process safely.

Season as you wish and stir until the meat is just browning.

Turn on the heat under your canner, leaving it open. Then place your canning lids in a small saucepan full of water and turn on the heat. Bring to simmering, then hold the lids in the hot water until you need them.

Now, with a slotted spoon, scoop up the meat and pack into your jars, to within an inch of the top of the jar. This leaves an inch of headspace. After all the jars have been packed, add enough water to the frying pan to make a broth to fill your jars. I sometimes add powdered beef soup stock to this broth to make it more "beefy" tasting. This is not necessary, though. When the broth is boiling, ladle it out and pour it into each jar, filling it to within an inch of the top of the jar.

Wipe the rim of each jar quickly with a clean damp cloth to remove any grease or meat particles. Place your hot, previously simmered lid on the jar and screw down the ring firmly tight. Place the hot jars into your hot canner, being careful not to bang them together. When all your jars have been placed in the canner, put on the lid and tighten it down. Leave the pressure weight off or leave the petcock(s) open, depending on the brand of canner you are using. Turn up the heat under the canner.

You must let the canner heat up and exhaust steam. This generally takes about ten minutes, although it can take longer when you have many jars in it. You want the steam to be exhausting forcibly, not just puttering out in little spurts and spits.

Meat must be canned at 10 pounds pressure, unless you live at an altitude above 1,000 feet above sea level. If you do, you must adjust your pressure to suit your altitude. (See the chart on page 50.)

Pints and half-pints of pork, beef and venison, including moose and elk meat, should be processed for 75 minutes, and quarts must be processed for 90 minutes.

When the time for processing the meat is up, immediately turn off the heat under the canner or remove the canner from the heat.

Let the pressure gauge return to zero or when using a weight gauge, let the canner cool for about 10 minutes, then gently nudge the weight. If it is still under pressure, a little spurt of steam will escape. If this happens, let it cool more. When no steam spurts out, remove the weight and open the canner carefully. Use caution when lifting the canner lid, as there is always more steam in it that will escape right into your face unless you're careful.

Immediately lift out the jars with your jar lifter, and set them on a dry, folded towel out of any drafts. Setting a hot jar in a draft can cause cracking or a failed seal. Keep the jars an inch or two apart to allow for quick and thorough cooling, as this helps the jars to seal well.

As the jars seal, the lids will "boing" and "ping" intermittently. The liquid in the jars will still be vigorously boiling. This is normal. Do not poke at or even touch the lids while they are sealing; it can cause seals to fail. After the jars are cool to the touch, check the seals. A tight, dipped in the center lid is sealed. One that pushes down, then pops back up is not sealed. Refrigerate or re-process unsealed jars right away, using a new hot, previously simmered lid. Inspect any jar that doesn't seal for a tiny crack in the rim of the jar, often this is the reason they don't seal.

Canning roasts or steaks

I home can many jars of different varieties of roast and steak. Now when I say "steak," this is wonderful meat, tasty and tender. But it is not "steak" as in fresh meat, fried or grilled. This steak I use in recipes like Swiss steak or mushroom steak, where you heat it with a sauce. I will admit that I do get hungry for a fried or grilled piece of fresh meat long before hunting season. And as I have no freezer, by choice, I either have to buy a piece of meat or trade a friend for one.

To can up your roasts, simply cut meat across the grain, then slice them into pieces just a little larger than will go raw into your canning jars. Like the stewing meat, it's best to brown and partially precook the roast. It seals in the moisture and flavor, and it lets the meat shrink down so that you can fit more into a canning jar.

I use a large frying pan to sear several pieces of roast at a time, carefully turning each one so all sides get evenly browned. Then I lift them out and stack them into a roasting pan. When it contains all the meat I will be processing at one batch, I add water and possibly some powdered beef stock to the frying pan and stir up the brown crusts, left from the frying. This I pour into the roasting pan, with the pieces of precooked meat, adding more water if I think it won't be enough to cover the meat in the jars. I put the lid on the roaster and cook for just long enough to shrink the meat down a little.

You may use any seasonings you prefer at this point.

When you figure the meat is about half done, lift it out into your clean canning jars and pack them to within an inch of the top. Here again, I cover the meat with broth, to an inch of the top of the jar, taking care to work out any air bubbles. I use a chopstick, but you can use a small spatula or wooden knife, too. From here on, you process the roasts and steaks just like you did the stewing meat.

Processing ground meat

I probably can more ground meat, both alone and in recipes, than any other form of meat. This is because you have more of it when you butcher an animal, and because it is so versatile. You just use ground meat in so many dishes.

Now you *can* make hamburger patties, using very low fat hamburger, lightly brown them, then pack them into widemouthed jars and process them with little or no liquid. But when you take them out to use them, the texture is *not* like that of a hamburger, but more like meatloaf. It is a smoother, more compact texture that some people don't like in a hamburger bun. It depends on your family's taste. I do use this method, but when I take the meat out, I arrange it on cookie sheets, put some catsup or barbecue sauce on it, diced onions and slices of green pepper and bake it. You now have little "personal sized" meatloaves that you can then slip onto a bun.

Most often, I simply lightly fry up the lean ground meat and either season it (as for taco filling), or not, as I want. This is one time I do mark the tops of my jars; I want to know what flavorings are in my burger.

When we home can ground meat, I always either buy the leanest burger I can get, or if it is hunted or home raised, I grind it with very little fat. When we grind venison, I mix a little beef fat with it, both for texture and taste. Some people grind pork with the venison, but I think it tastes better with the beef tallow in it, in limited amounts.

If you can any fatty meat at all, you run the risk of having your lids not seal as the fat can get between the lid and the rim of the jar during processing. This is why I severely trim all meat I am going to can and why I grind very little fat with my ground meat. Besides, less fat is healthier for your heart.

With any of your ground beef, you may season it beforehand, as you cook it down, or you may leave it unseasoned and season it when you use it. Go light with the seasoning, however, as canning will strengthen the taste of the spices. You can always add more when you go to use it.

You can also can your own meatballs, with or without sauce. These are very good and extra handy. Simply make your favorite meatball recipe and roll your balls into a golf ball size or smaller. Lightly brown them in very little oil. While they are cooking, gently turn each one so they brown evenly on all sides. Then, carefully pack them into wide-mouth jars.

Pack the meatballs hot into hot jars, to within an inch of the top. Ladle broth or a tomato sauce over the meatballs. I've also had good luck using cream of mushroom soup, diluted with broth or water. Do not use thick, flour-thickened gravy, because it may cause the meat to not heat sufficiently for safe processing.

Remove all air bubbles possible and process at 10 pounds pressure (see altitude chart on page 50) for 75 minutes for pints and 90 minutes for quarts.

As with all meat, I've found it is best to cover the meat with broth made from the brownings and water. It makes it heat equally during processing and keeps the meat moist and tender. You may use this, or add tomato sauce (seasoned as you wish), and a bit of water, heated to boiling, to cover your ground meat in the jars. Just remember to put hot meat into the jars, and quickly cover it to within an inch of the top of the jar with your hot broth/sauce.

Raw packing steaks and chops

Small steaks and chops, such as pork chops, lamb chops, and veal chops can be raw packed if you wish. They may have small bones left in, which adds to the flavor of the meat during processing. I do not do this with venison, as it is the fat and the bones that often give venison a "gamey" taste. Remove all venison fat and bones before canning steaks or chops.

Cut the meat into one inch slices, removing any large bones. Pack into hot, widemouth jars to within an inch of the top of the jar. You may add ½ tsp. salt to pints and 1 tsp. to quarts for flavor, if you wish. Immediately fill jar to within an inch of the top with hot broth. You may use powdered beef or pork stock or else boil a batch of bones, skim off the fat, remove the bones, and use this broth in your canning.

Remove air bubbles and process jars at 10 pounds pressure (see altitude requirement chart) for 75 minutes for pints and 90 minutes for quarts.

Canning pork sausage

When you are going to homecan your own ground pork sausage, make your favorite recipe as you grind the pork, but omit the sage as it sometimes tastes awful when canned. When you go to reheat it for use, simply sprinkle a little sage onto the patties while simmering with a lid on and they will quickly absorb the sage flavor.

To can pork sausage patties, simply make your patties just a little larger than your widemouth jars and lightly brown them in little oil. Pack hot sausage into hot jars, leaving an inch of headroom. Pour hot broth over the sausages, again leaving an inch of headroom. Remove any air bubbles. Process the same as all above meat.

Pepperoni and salami

Believe it or not, you can easily can pepperoni or salami, or most any other dry sausage. To can whole dry sausages, like pepperoni, simply cut a chunk that will fill your jar to within an inch of the top of the jar, place a hot, previously simmered lid on it and process it for 75 minutes for pints, at 10 pounds pressure. If you live at an altitude above 1,000 feet, see the altitude chart for adjusting the pressure, if necessary. So simple!

Sliced dry sausages, such as pepperoni, is just as easy. Just pack your sliced meat into pint or half-pint jars, to an inch from the top of the jar, cap and process, the same as with whole sausage. No sweat! I just canned 38 half-pints of sliced pepperoni that I got for a great deal; it was nearly to its freshness date. Now it's good forever, despite power outages, ice storms, floods, or hurricanes.

With these sausages, fat will be cooked out of them, ending up in the bottom of the jar. Leave the fat behind when you use the sausages—the taste is the same, but there will be much less grease to clog your arteries.

Small game

Rabbits or any small game animals can be easily home canned. If there is quite a bit of damage from gunshot, soak for an hour in a salt brine, made with a gallon of water and 4 Tbsp. salt stirred up in it. Soak, then rinse and pat dry.

I prefer to hot pack my small meats as you get more meat into a jar and there is less wasted space. When you raw pack meat it shrinks during the processing, and you end up with a lot of extra space in each jar.

I usually boil or bake the whole rabbit, squirrels, or whatever until it is nearly done. Then I remove the meat from the bones and pack it into jars. You can also disjoint the meat and pack it with the bones in. Pack the meat into hot jars, leaving an inch of headroom. Pour hot water or hot broth over the meat, also leaving an inch of headroom. Remove all bubbles. Add a ½ tsp. salt to pints and 1 tsp. to quarts, if desired.

For bone-in meat, process at 10 pounds pressure (see altitude chart) for 65 minutes for pints and 75 minutes for quarts. For deboned meat, process at 10 pounds pressure (see altitude chart) for 75 minutes for pints and 90 minutes for quarts. The reason for this difference is that with small animals, the meat is thinner and with bone-in meat, there is more room for the hot broth to penetrate quickly, heating the meat faster than if you are canning boned meat, which is packed in tighter.

I've found that my kids were much happier eating the rabbits they raised and wild game they hunted a few months after it was killed. The sentiment had worn off by then, and I didn't make an issue of what was for dinner. We just ate it and were thankful.

Home canning poultry

While I have raw packed poultry, I have found that it is much nicer and more efficient to hot pack it. Here you precook the meat and pack it hot into hot jars. When I raw packed my chickens that we were butchering in a hurry, the canning went fast. But when it was finished, there was a whole lot of jar and not so much meat left down in the bottom of it, and the end product did not look appetizing as it does with hot packed poultry. Another drawback is that the raw packed poultry tended to be a little chewy after processing and storage, as it kind of dried out. So today I do nearly all my poultry using the hot pack method.

You may use these directions for any poultry, fowl, or game birds.

Boil or bake the birds until nearly done, so the meat will pull easily off the bones. I prefer to remove the bones and boil them up for broth to cover the meat. In this way, no space in the jar is taken up by bones.

I pack my poultry into both pint and half-pint jars. The widemouth pints contain whole or large pieces of breast. If you have a large family, you may want to use widemouth quarts for the same choice pieces of meat. Regular jars can hold the large pieces of meat from the legs and thighs. Or you can dice all the leftover meat into them. This is handy to use for a huge assortment of recipes. In the store, less than a half-pint of diced chicken breast is over $2.

I usually remove the breasts and can those in large pieces or whole, depending on the size of the birds. The rest of the bird I dice up, as I use a whole lot of diced poultry meat in mixed recipes from chicken enchiladas to chicken noodle soup.

Like I said, I boil or steam the bird, debone it, and pack it into hot jars. Then I ladle the grease off the broth and pour the broth over the meat, to within an inch of the top of the jars. Remove air bubbles. This boned meat is processed at 10 pounds pressure (see altitude chart) for 75 minutes for pints and 90 minutes for quarts. Bone-in poultry meat is processed for less time due to the spacing the bones create, allowing the meat to heat quicker and more thoroughly. This is processed at 10 pounds pressure (see altitude chart) for 65 minutes for pints and 75 minutes for quarts.

One reason I like to bone my poultry is that it leaves me with this big pile of bones and a lot of extra broth for making a soup base. I put the bones back in the broth. With a baked turkey, I add water to the roasting pan, mix in the brownings and pour the works in a large stock pot with the turkey carcass or bones. I simmer all the bones for about half an hour, then let it cool down so I can handle the bones. I carefully remove any clinging meat on the bones and put it into a bowl. I put the bones into another bowl and "yucky" scraps into another for the huskies' treats. **Never feed cooked small bones, such as poultry or pork bones to dogs. It can kill them by puncturing their intestines.** I skim most of the fat off the cooled broth and add that to the huskies' dry food. Then I take the little bit of shredded meat I have and put it into several pint or quart jars. I heat up the broth again to boiling, adding some powdered chicken soup base or seasonings, as I like. While that's heating, I often add a small handful of grated carrots, perhaps a few peas, parsley or whatever I want, a handful of rice or dry noodles, then add the broth to within an inch of the top of the jar. Process at 10 pounds pressure (see altitude chart) for 75 minutes (pints) or 90 minutes (quarts). I usually use regular mouth quart jars, since I usually use a quart of this ready-made soup base at a time.

A few last hints

Use a broth on your meat, not a heavy gravy. Thick, flour thickened gravies canned with your meat could prevent the meat from quickly heating thoroughly while processing.

Always wipe the rim of your jars after filling, with a warm, damp, clean cloth. Grease on a jar rim is your enemy; it can prevent the jars from sealing.

If a jar does not seal, reprocess it with a new, previously simmered lid right away, or refrigerate until you can. (Reheat it before you again put it into your canner.) If it's a single jar and you're through canning, simply use it soon in a home-cooked meal.

Always check a jar before you re-heat it to use. Make sure the seal is still firmly indented in the center and that you have to really pry to remove the lid. If it comes off easily it's not sealed. Now look at the contents. Do they look appetizing and normal? Does the meat smell great? Before tasting the meat, heat it to boiling temperature for 10-15 minutes (longer for altitudes above 1,000 feet) before tasting or serving. You do not have to boil the meat, but make sure you heat it to boiling temperature which ever way you prepare it, be it in a casserole, a stew, roasted in the oven, etc. By doing this every time you use a jar of your home canned meat, you will ensure that you and your family are safe from food poisoning.

Always read your canning manual before attempting to can anything. It's only common sense.

I hope you are off on the road to a whole new way of food storage. While many people home can pickles, jams, and jellies, not so many attempt meats. And because they're so good and easy to can, they're missing a whole lot. So, try putting up some meat. You'll soon discover how truly indispensable they are! Good canning! 🐾

Canning meals in a jar

By Jackie Clay

While some canning is "seasonal," which means that you put up what you have just harvested as soon as it becomes ripe, there's a whole different canning season that is less demanding and lets you convert meats and vegetables in your freezer or root cellar into quick and easy meals. Just dump out a jar or two and you've got a home cooked meal without waiting. I don't know how many times I've used these convenience foods on my pantry shelves. When you have a busy homestead, you often are outside working and suddenly it's past lunch time and not only are you hungry, but your family is hungry too. Not "sandwich hungry." Hungry! And you don't have time to roast a chicken, make a stew, bake a casserole. So instead of resorting to store-bought food in a can, how about using some of your own "instant meals?"

Late winter and early spring are perfect times to do this, as some of your stored vegetables are trying to go soft on you. Are your onions sprouting greens? Are your potatoes sprouting sprouts? Are your carrots kind of shriveling? Rutabagas wrinkling? Before they get to the stage where you sigh and carry them out to the pigs, how about turning them into some scrumptious quick meals-in-a-jar?

You can even use some of your own home canned tomato sauce, poultry, beef, venison, and broth to concoct these recipes. How about using some of your long-term storage foods, such as dried beans and rice so you can rotate them as you should. And did you know that dried beans tend to get so old that they don't want to cook up tender without long cooking? Before they get to that stage, use them to make your daily cooking faster, with less work and bother.

Do you have meat in the freezer that is getting nearly a year old and is in danger of becoming freezer burned? Freezer burn is that whitish "frostbite" on your frozen meat that gives it a terrible smell and awful taste. It's caused by oxygen getting into your packages and is pretty much irreversible. Before this happens, you can easily thaw the meat and use it in making your meals-in-a-jar. In this way, it won't be wasted, doesn't require more thought and you'll appreciate it every time you open a jar and feed your family.

While I'm going to give you plenty of recipes and tips, these aren't the only foods you can home can as quick meals. Just about any family recipe can be home canned. But there are a few cautions here:

1. Don't can a very thick product, such as one with thick gravy, lots of rice, or pasta. This can cause a problem because the heat during processing cannot penetrate evenly into the entire contents of the jar and could cause incomplete processing and possible food poisoning.

2. When you can up a mixed recipe, always process it for the longest time (and method) required for the ingredient that requires more stringent processing, usually meat or poultry. For instance, say you're making up a batch of beef stew to can and will be adding potatoes, carrots, onions, tomatoes, and stewing beef. You must process pints for 75 minutes and quarts for 90 minutes, regardless that say, carrots, require only 30 minutes processing.

3. Always take into consideration that you *must* pressure can *all* recipes that contain meat, vegetables, and poultry, including their broths. These are all low acid foods, requiring pressure canning. Period. No "My grandma used to can it in a water bath canner." You *must* pressure can all low acid foods and combinations thereof.

4. When pressure canning, most recipes say "10 pounds pressure" as a starting point. This is for folks who live at altitudes of 1,000 feet above sea level and lower. If you live at a higher altitude, you must adjust your

pressure to suit your altitude. (We all know that potatoes take longer to cook, the higher you are; same difference with canning.)

I know I mention this altitude adjustment in just about everything I write about home canning, but still people miss it and wonder why, when they live at 6,000 feet and can at 10 pounds pressure, they have some foods that do not keep in their pantries! Altitude adjustment is not optional; it's necessary.

Okay, lets get to making some good old convenience foods, right at home in our kitchen.

Beef stew (also venison stew):

My son, David, eating home-canned sloppy joes and baked beans. I made the buns with half-time spoon roll recipe, (Backwoods Home Magazine, Nov/Dec 2007, Issue #108. Also available in Backwoods Home Cooking, page 37) plus a little more flour, topped with spices. Not bad.

5 pounds beef or venison stew meat
1 Tbsp. oil
3 qts. cubed potatoes
2 qts. sliced or cut carrots
3 cups chopped celery
3 cups chopped onions
1 quart or more tomato sauce or stewed tomatoes (optional)
1½ Tbsp. salt
½ tsp. black pepper

Cut meat into 1 inch cubes; brown in oil. Combine meat, vegetables, and seasonings in a large stock pot and cover with tomato sauce, tomatoes, or water and bring to a boil. Do not cook. Ladle hot stew into hot jars, leaving 1 inch headroom. Remove any air bubbles. Wipe jar rim clean, put hot, previously simmered lid on jar and screw down ring firmly tight. Process pints for 75 minutes and quarts for 90 minutes at 10 pounds pressure. Makes about 14 pints or 7 quarts.

Chili con carne:

5 pounds ground meat (beef or venison)
2 cups chopped onions
1 clove garlic, minced
6 quarts canned tomatoes w/juice
3 cups dry kidney beans
1 quart tomato sauce (optional)
½ cup chili powder
1 sweet green bell pepper, seeded and chopped
1½ Tbsp. salt
1 red jalepeño pepper, seeded and chopped finely (I use 2 dry, smoked chipotle peppers

The morning you are going to make your chili to can, rinse the beans, and pick out stones and bad beans. Cover with water three times as deep as the beans and bring to a boil. Boil 5 minutes, then remove from heat, cover and let stand for at least 2 hours. When ready to make chili, continue by browning meat in a large kettle. (I omit this when using home canned meat.) In place of ground meat, you can also make chunky chili by using stewing meat instead of the ground meat.

Add remaining ingredients, draining beans, and simmer for 20 minutes to blend flavors. Ladle hot chili into hot jars. Wipe jar rims clean, place hot, previously simmered lids on jars and screw down rings firmly tight. Process pints 75 minutes and quarts for 90 minutes at 10 pounds pressure.

Hint: Take it easy on the "hot." As you can the chili, it intensifies. You can always add more heat later, when you heat the chili to serve; you can't remove too much spiciness.

Meatballs in sauce:

5 lbs. ground meat (beef or venison)
3 cups cracker crumbs
5 eggs
3 cups chopped onion
1 sweet green pepper (optional)
1½ tsp. salt
½ tsp. pepper
Variety 1 uses 3 pints tomato sauce
Variety 2 uses 1 family size can cream of mushroom soup + 1 can water

For both varieties, mix ground meat, cracker crumbs, beaten eggs, onion, pepper, and seasonings. Then form into meatballs the size of a golf ball. Gently brown in a large frying pan with minimal oil. Turn as needed to brown evenly.

With variety 1, heat tomato sauce to boiling, with variety 2 pour mushroom soup and water into frying pan with meat drippings and heat, stirring well to mix in drippings.

Pack hot meatballs gently into hot wide mouth pint or quart jars to within an inch of the top, then ladle on hot sauce to just cover the meatballs to within an inch of headroom. Carefully wipe jar rim clean, put on hot, previously simmered lids and screw down rings firmly tight. Process pints for 75 minutes and quarts for 90 minutes at 10 pounds pressure.

Hint: To serve, you can simply put meatballs into a saucepan and heat, serve over noodles or in a quick casserole. They are very convenient as well as tasty.

Shredded barbecued beef:

5 pounds lean beef or venison roast or 5 pints canned lean meat (chunks or stew meat)

3 cups chopped onion

2 pints barbecue sauce (homemade or store bought of your choice of flavors)

Day one, roast your meat at 300° F with a cover on it and enough water to keep it from drying out or scorching; if you've got a crock pot, use that if you like. Remove from heat and cool.

Cut meat across the grain so that it's only an inch thick. Then pull the meat apart, shredding it and removing any fat, etc. Add onion and barbecue sauce. Add enough broth from the roasting/canning, to thin the sauce considerably; you don't want this too thick to can. Simmer until onion is nearly tender and well mixed; add a bit of water if you need to, to keep from scorching. Stir frequently. Ladle hot into hot pint jars, wipe rims well, and place hot, previously simmered lid on jar and screw down ring firmly tight. Process pints for 75 minutes and quarts for 90 minutes.

This is so handy when guests pop in. You've got "instant" barbecue beef sandwich material. Just heat and spoon on the rolls.

Chicken noodle (or rice) soup:

4 quarts chicken stock (boil up one good sized chicken)

3 cups diced chicken

1½ cups diced celery

1½ cups sliced or grated (medium holes) carrots

1 cup chopped onion

dry thick noodles or rice

seasonings to taste (no sage; often gets bitter on canning)

salt to taste

Boil up chicken, cool, remove bones, dice up meat, and strain stock through a sieve to remove debris. Combine stock, chicken, vegetables, and seasonings into a large pot and bring to a boil. Simmer 20 minutes. You may also add chicken soup base powder or 3 bouillon cubes if you wish. Ladle hot soup into hot jars, filling half full. Add a handful of noodles or rice to each quart jar; half for pints, and ladle soup in leaving 1 inch headroom. Do not add more noodles or rice, or your end product will be too thick. Wipe rim of jar clean, place hot, previously simmered lid on jar and screw down ring firmly tight. Process pints 75 minutes and quarts 90 minutes at 10 pounds pressure.

Boston baked beans:

> 2 quarts dried navy or great
>   northern beans
> 1 pound thick sliced bacon or salt pork, cut into small pieces
> 6 large onions, diced
> 1½ cups brown sugar
> 4 tsp. salt
> 4 tsp. dry mustard
> 1^1/3 cups molasses

Sort beans, rinse, then cover with 6 quarts of fresh water; let stand over night in a cool place. Drain. Cover beans with 6 quarts water in a large stock pot. Bring beans to a boil; reduce heat. Cover and simmer until skins begin to crack. Drain, reserving liquid. Pour beans into a turkey roaster or other large baking dish. Add bacon/pork and onions. Combine remaining ingredients and 8 cups reserved bean liquid (add water to make 8 cups if necessary). Ladle sauce over beans. Cover; bake at 350° F for about 3 hours. Add water if necessary; beans should be watery not dry. Pack hot beans and sauce into hot jars, leaving 1 inch of headroom. Remove any air bubbles. Wipe rims clean, put on hot, previously simmered lids, and screw down rings firmly tight. Process pints for 80 minutes and quarts for 95 minutes at 10 pounds pressure.

This makes homemade baked beans an "instant" food like store bought bacon and beans but that's oh so much better. It also uses your stored dry beans before they get too old and "gets rid" of onions before they go soft.

Do you like your baked beans with a tomato based sauce, kind of like some store brands? Easy to do, too; here is a recipe for that style of baked beans.

Pork and beans with tomato sauce:

2 quarts dried navy or great northern beans
½ pound of bacon or salt pork, cut into pieces
2 cups chopped onion
8 Tbsp. brown sugar
½ tsp. allspice
½ tsp. ground cloves
1 quart tomato juice

Cover beans and let stand overnight. Drain. Cover beans with boiling water by 4 inches in a large stock pot. Boil 3 minutes. Remove from heat and let stand 10 minutes. Drain. Combine other ingredients except the pork. Bring to a boil. Pack 1 cup of beans into hot jars; top with a piece of pork/bacon; fill jar ¾ full with beans and add another piece of pork. Then ladle hot sauce over beans leaving 1 inch of headroom. Remove any air bubbles, wipe rim clean, place hot, previously simmered lid on jar and screw down ring firmly tight. Process pints for 65 minutes and quarts for 75 minutes at 10 pounds pressure.

Chicken a la king:

1 large chicken boiled down in 3 quarts of water
4 level Tbsp. flour
1 Tbsp. salt
1 pint canned mushrooms
1 chopped green bell pepper
2 chopped pimiento peppers or red sweet bell peppers
1 cup chopped onion
1 tsp. black pepper

Cut chicken into pieces and add 3 quarts water and cook in a large pot until tender. Cool, remove meat from bones, and cut into small pieces. Dissolve flour and salt in a little of the cold broth, making a paste. Add the remainder of the broth, making 1 quart total broth. Cook until slightly thickened. Add mushrooms, peppers, onions, and chicken meat. Heat to boiling but do not boil. Ladle immediately into hot jars. Remove any air bubbles, wipe rim clean, place hot, previously simmered lid on jar, and screw down ring firmly tight. Process pints for 75 minutes and quarts for 90 minutes at 10 pounds pressure.

This makes a very quick meal when company comes or you are really hungry. I can whip up a batch of fresh biscuits in a few minutes and while the chicken a la king is heating up, the biscuits are baking. What a great "instant" meal.

Another different chicken based meal is Brunswick stew. You won't find that in any store and it's really good on a cold day. I often make it with end of the year tomatoes as they get less and less as I put them up. This doesn't use a whole lot, and it makes something different with them. Give it a try.

Brunswick stew:

¼ pound thick sliced bacon

1 chicken

2 cups water

1 cup potatoes, cubed

1 quart tomatoes with juice

2 cups butter beans

2 Tbsp. onion, chopped fine

1½ cups okra (optional)

4 tsp. salt

1 Tbsp. sugar

½ lemon, sliced thin

1 tsp. celery seed

½ tsp. ground cloves

1 tsp. pepper

¼ tsp. cayenne pepper

Cut bacon in cubes and fry until crisp and brown. Cut chicken into pieces, put into frying pan with water. Cook slowly until chicken falls from bones; adding more water if necessary to prevent scorching. Remove chicken from bones. Add chopped vegetables and rest of ingredients. Bring to a boil and pack hot into hot jars to within an inch of the top of the jar. Wipe rim clean and place hot, previously simmered lid on jar and screw down ring firmly tight. Process pints for 75 minutes and quarts for 90 minutes at 10 pounds pressure.

Brunswick stew is a "different" instant meal. You can add spices to your own taste, if you wish.

Swiss steak with mushroom sauce:

several cubed steaks or round steak cut 1 inch thick, cut into pieces to fit into wide
   mouthed jars
6 Tbsp. oil
2 Tbsp. flour
1 pint cold water, or more
1 Tbsp. salt
2 cups mushrooms, cut into pieces
2 sweet red peppers, cut fine

Add oil to large frying pan and brown meat without scorching. Remove the meat to a warm place. Add flour to frying pan, stirring well and add cold water gradually to make a *thin* gravy. Add salt, mushrooms, and peppers. Bring to a boil. Pack steak pieces into hot jars to within an inch of the top and ladle the mushroom sauce over them to within an inch of the top also. Wipe the rim clean, add hot, previously simmered lids on jars and screw down ring firmly tight. Process pints for 75 minutes and quarts for 90 minutes at 10 pounds pressure.

Heat this up when you need a quick meal, add some of your own vegetables, and you have a "company meal" in 15 minutes.

There are literally dozens and dozens more "instant" meals you can home can. These will give you an idea. Be sure to follow safe canning practices and always have a canning manual on hand, just to be sure. I always do this, even though I've been canning for a long time. I don't want to make a stupid mistake and we're all capable of that.

One hint I want to pass along is that I have a whole lot of meats and poultry canned up. With these as a base, it takes no time at all to put together a good meal. After all, the meat has already been cooked. For instance, I can slip a turkey breast fillet out of a jar, cut up a few potatoes, add a jar of carrots, and make a nice quick stuffing and in less than 20 minutes I can serve a nice turkey dinner. And it's chemical free, cheap, and above all, very tasty.

Give "meals in a jar" a try and see if you don't agree. They're the best. ❧

Canned salmon

By Linda Gabris

One of the most versatile items on the pantry shelf is a can of salmon. It can be the ingredient in a platter of enticing appetizers, an elegant creamy mousse, or pan full of savory patties for a quick and satisfying supper. Even something as simple as a salmon sandwich can become gourmet when the quality of the fish is top-notch, but choice canned salmon is expensive. The good news is, you can can your own.

It's true that canning fish is serious business. Nevertheless, salmon lovers who are willing to follow instructions carefully can master the technique of canning their own fish, whether it's a personal catch or just reeled in fresh from the supermarket at too good of a price to pass up.

The only safe way to can fish is by the pressure canning method. Open-kettle, steam, oven, boiling water, or other canning practices that our grandmothers gambled with are not recommended. As complicated as it sounds, preserving food by pressure canning is a simple act of sterilizing food under heated pressure using proven time and temperature to halt the growth of microorganisms like molds or yeasts as well as to deactivate the enzymes that cause decay.

As food in the jar is heated, the contents expand and pressure increases significantly, causing air to vent from the jar. After processing, the atmospheric pressure outside the jar is greater than inside and this difference causes the lid to be sucked down onto the jar creating a vacuum seal. When air is locked out of the jar, harmful bacteria does not get a chance to grow and contaminate food inside.

Once you have a dependable pressure canner, the first step calls for top-quality ingredients. A fish cannot come out of the jar in any better shape than it goes in. You need to have fresh, firm fish to produce optimum results. I have canned good buys on frozen salmon and found they do up quite well, but for gourmet fare nothing beats fish fresh out of the water. If you are doing fish already frozen, thaw it completely in the fridge before proceeding.

Preparing salmon for the jar is an act of personal preference. I have no use for heads, tails, fins, backbones, or belly fat in my favorite recipes so I get rid of these undesirables. When fish are trimmed to suit your own liking, cut into one or two-inch chunks. Previously-frozen fish should be soaked in brine made up of two cups of salt per gallon of cold water. Soak for 20 minutes to draw out excess blood and to help firm up the flesh before cutting. I find that fresh salmon do not need to be soaked. Rinse well and pat with paper towels to remove traces of slime and other liquid. The salmon are now ready to pack into prepared jars.

Use only Mason or approved canning jars which are freshly fitted with brand new snap lids and screw-on bands that are in good condition. Never use nicked jars and recycled lids for any food, especially fish. Jars with wire bails, rubber band seals, glass or one-piece zinc or porcelain-lined caps should not be used. Inspect jars carefully and throw away any with faults or chips. Wash in hot soapy water, rinse well, and scald. Boil snap lids five minutes to soften

Elegant salmon mousse makes great party fare

the sealing compound. Remove from the heat but keep in hot water until ready to use.

Pack the salmon tightly, skin side out (if left on) into hot, clean jars. I usually process mine in 250 ml (half-pint) jars which are sold special-ly for canning salmon. After the fish is packed into the jar, leaving ¼-inch headspace, add ½ teaspoon of salt. Contrary to what some folks might believe, salt does not play a role in preserving when using the pressure canning method. It is merely used as seasoning, so if you are on a low or no salt diet, you can omit it.

Next, drizzle two teaspoons of white vinegar into each jar. Vinegar is added to help soften and break down the bones during processing. At this point you can stray a little and be creative. Some of my canning acquaintances confess to adding a teaspoon or two of ketchup to each jar for color. I have found that a few drops of Tabasco sauce also enhances color while adding a distinctive zip, as does a pinch of fra-grant sweet paprika. A bay leaf, a few peppercorns, or a drop of sesame or olive oil can be added for a unique flavor. Do not add any other liq-uid as the fish will release its own juice during the canning process.

Use a rubber spatula to remove air bubbles. Now, dab a dish cloth into scalding water, then dip into vinegar and wipe jar rims thoroughly. This important step of removing any trace particles will ensure a good seal. Center the lids on the jars. Apply the screw bands and tighten until just lightly tight. Do not over-tighten.

When the jars are filled, put into the pressure canner and add three quarts of water or amount recommended in your own manual. Lock the lid into place and bring to a boil until steam escapes from the control valve. At this point, vent the canner to allow steam to escape steadily for 10 minutes (or follow the recommendations in your canner's manu-al). This step allows all air to be removed from inside the cooker to ensure correct canning.

Now, close the valve. When the canner reaches the recommended pressure for the size of jar and altitude, begin counting the processing time. For half pint jars, mine calls for 100 minutes. Be sure to time exactly. You must strive to maintain uniform pressure and never let your steam gauge show more than 20 pounds of pressure. If this happens, release enough steam through vent to reduce pressure and then adjust the stove setting.

After the processing time is complete, remove the canner from the heat. Let it stand undisturbed until the pressure drops to zero. Wait three minutes, unscrew, and remove the cover. Slowly lift the jars from the canner and place on a towel in a draft-free place to cool. Do not re-tighten screw bands. Leave for 24 hours without disturbing.

When cool, you must check the seals very carefully. Unscrew the metal bands and store away for future use. Some homecanners leave the metal bands on, but it is easier to detect spoiled food when they are removed as any traces of bubbling over will be more visible. Properly sealed lids curve downward and will not flex when pressed. If you find any unsealed jars, either refrigerate and use as soon as possible, reprocess, or empty the fish into a zip-lock bag and freeze.

Label the sealed jars and store in a cool, dark place. It is recommended that home canned foods be used within one year. If you fancy canned salmon as much as I do and depend on it to impress your company with tasty appetizers, make a delectable sandwich, or super supper you'll never have to worry about a batch outliving its shelf life. Try the recipes below for some real treats.

Grandma's old-fashioned golden salmon patties: I've always had a passion for salmon patties and this old recipe is still one of my favorites.

1 pint jar drained salmon (save juice)

2 cups cold mashed potatoes

½ cup finely minced onion

2 eggs

¼ cup of saved juice

salt, pepper, celery salt to taste

fine bread crumbs

Mix all ingredients, except crumbs. If too dry, add some more of the saved juice. Using hands, form into patties. Roll in crumbs. Sauté in oil or butter until crisp and golden. Serve hot with Tartar sauce. These patties make great fish burgers when served on buns with trimmings. Makes four to six.

Pink salmon mousse:

1 cup of salmon
2 envelopes of gelatin
½ cup liquid drained off the salmon
½ cup white wine
1 cup sour cream
¼ cup each finely minced red pepper, celery, and onion
½ tsp. very finely grated lemon rind
1 cup whipping cream
salt, pepper, and dill (fresh or dried) to taste

Place the salmon juice in a bowl over hot water and sprinkle on gelatin to soften. Stir in the wine. Chill until the mixture begins to thicken. Blend in the sour cream. Add the minced vegetables, lemon rind, and flaked salmon. Whip the cream until stiff and fold it gently into the gelatin mixture. Season with salt, pepper, and dill. Pour into a lightly oiled mold and chill until firm. Unmold and garnish as desired. Makes about eight cups. This makes a very attractive and tasty buffet dish.

Variation: Cut four lemons in half and scoop out the centers. (Save the pulp for lemonade or pie filling). Cut the edges of the lemon shells in decorative fashion.

Lemon shells filled with salmon mousse. They make wonderful appetizers easy when there's home-canned salmon in the pantry.

Pat dry with paper towels and fill with the mousse. Garnish with parsley or capers. Serve as appetizers. You'll have enough mousse left over to pile on crackers as an extra treat.

Salmon Dip:

1 cup canned salmon
1 cup sour cream
3 Tbsp. ketchup
3 Tbsp. sweet pickle relish
1 Tbsp. sesame oil
1 tsp. horseradish
2 tsp. lemon juice
3 Tbsp. minced chives
shake or two of Tabasco sauce
½ tsp. seasoned salt
fresh, minced parsley

Mix all the ingredient except the parsley in a bowl. Form into a ball with oiled hands and roll the ball in the parsley until it's coated. Refrigerate for at least two hours before serving. Makes about four cups of delicious dip that goes great with carrot sticks, celery stalks, cauliflower, broccoli, or crisp crackers. 🦐

Pickles and relishes

By Linda Gabris

When I was a kid, my grandparents had one of the biggest gardens in the countryside and, come autumn, there was nothing I enjoyed more than helping Grandma "put up" bushels of canned goods to stock the cellar shelves for winter use.

Of course, in those days, putting food by—or canning—was an important way of life for we seldom went to town in wintertime to shop for groceries. Every fall, Grandma and I did up enough mouthwatering goodies to carry us all the way through to the next year's harvest.

Even though today, unlike grandma, I have easy access to year-round shopping, I still take great pleasure, pride, and comfort in doing up my own preserves and condiments, like pickles and relishes, from the bounty of my backyard garden.

To me, there is no greater joy than breaking open a sparkling jar of something from the cellar and boasting that, "Yes, indeed, it's homemade!" And, the good news is, there's no need to fret if you don't have a garden or if your veggie patch didn't produce enough surplus crop for canning as you can get reasonable buys on seasonal produce at local farmer's markets, roadside fruit and vegetable stands, or even in grocery stores to fill your sealers for winter.

As far as home canning goes, the rules have changed some since my younger days. Canning jars have been updated, and home canners today have a set of basic rules laid down by experts that we can follow to help ensure that food is canned safely and does not go bad.

Use only top-quality ingredients. Let's face it, if you make dill pickles out of sandy, wilted cukes, you can bet your bottom dollar that your pickles will be gritty and lacking in crispness.

Same goes for making corn relish out of moldy ears of corn. The finished product will not be blue-ribbon worthy. Harvest your vegetables when they are at a prime for picking—on canning morning—wash thoroughly, then hold in icy cold water.

For long-term storage, you must heat process ALL home-canned foods either by boiling water bath or in a pressure canner. High-acid foods such as the pickles and relishes in the recipes below—which have large amounts of acid added in the form of vinegar—can be safely processed in a boiling water bath.

Grandma's old-fashioned garlic-style dills:

Here's a pickle recipe that's hard to beat. Select uniformly sized, firm, fresh cucumbers. Grandma always said, "pick cukes in the morning and pickle before lunch if you want a really super pickle." This recipe can be halved, doubled, or tripled depending on the size of your crop. Let these pickles age for at least 3 weeks before cracking open a jar. Makes 8 quarts.

8 pounds pickling cucumbers
a large pan that holds enough water and ice to cover cukes (Grandma soaked hers
   in fresh-drawn ice-cold well water)
8 sprigs fresh dill
32 cloves whole peeled garlic
8 Tbsp. pickling salt
8 tsp. mixed pickling spice
8 cups white vinegar
8 cups water

Wash cucumbers and scrub lightly with vegetable brush to remove sand. Rinse under cold running water. Put cucumbers in large bowl and cover with water. Add ice and let stand for an hour if fresh picked. If cucumbers are older than a couple of hours from picking, let stand for at least 4 hours to firm up, adding ice as needed or keep in fridge underwater.

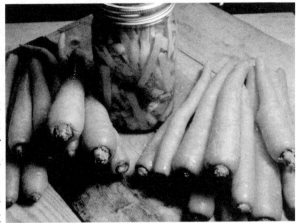

Make pickling liquid by mixing vinegar and water in large kettle and bringing to boil. Reduce heat and hold simmering while filling jars.

Spicy dilled carrots—a canned treat that's hard to beat

Remove jars from water. Place 1 sprig of dill, 4 cloves garlic, 1 tablespoon pickling salt, and 1 teaspoon pickling spice into each jar.

Pack cucumbers, standing upright. Add pickling liquid to cover, leaving headspace. If more liquid is needed, mix equal parts vinegar and water and bring to a boil.

Using spatula, remove air bubbles. Follow directions above for proceeding with boiling water bath. Process 15 minutes.

Spicy dilled carrots:

Great color and crunch for any pickle platter. Make one jar of super long sticks to use as cocktail stirrers. Makes 8 quarts.

7 pounds carrots
6 cups white vinegar
2 cups water
1 cup sugar
½ cup pickling salt
16 cloves garlic
8 sprigs dill
8 hot peppers (or 8 pinches of hot dried chili peppers)
2 Tbsp. pickling spice

Scrub carrots. Cut into desired-size sticks. Drop into icy water until all carrots are prepared.

Mix vinegar, water, sugar, and salt and bring to boil. Keep hot.

Put 2 cloves garlic, 1 sprig of dill, 1 hot pepper, or pinch of chili pepper and ¼ teaspoon pickling spice into each hot jar. Pack carrot sticks to within ¾" of rim. Add boiling brine to cover.

Remove air bubbles. Proceed as above for boiling water bath. Process 15 minutes.

Aunt Mernie's chunky mustard pickles:

The saying goes that Aunt Mernie got the recipe from Grandma, but over the years—after adding a pinch of this and a pinch of that—she perfected the pickles to the point where Grandma had to ask for the recipe back. Makes about 5 quarts or about 10 pint-sized jars.

2 quarts sliced cukes
(Grandma used chunks of peeled yellow, seeded garden cucumbers. Aunt Mernie used unpeeled pickling cukes cut into fours; perhaps that's why her pickles were so much more gourmet)
2 cups sliced onions (for gourmet use baby or pearl onions)
1 cauliflower, cut into small
   flowerets
2 sweet red peppers, cut into chunks
½ cup pickling salt
2 cups vinegar
1 cup water
3 cups sugar
2 tsp. celery seed
pinch each of ginger and curry powder
2 Tbsp. mustard powder
1 Tbsp. turmeric
¾ cup flour
1 cup water

Place cucumbers and onions in large bowl. Sprinkle with salt. Let stand one hour. While soaking, steam the cauliflower and peppers until barely tender. Drain.

Drain cucumbers and onions. Rinse under cold running water. Add cooked vegetables and mix well.

Place vinegar, water, and sugar in pot and heat to boiling. Whisk dry ingredients with water until smooth and slowly blend into vinegar mix, cooking until thick and smooth. Add vegetables and bring to a rolling boil.

Ladle into jars. Proceed as above for boiling water bath, processing 20 minutes.

Corn nugget relish:

So pretty, so good. In our house we use corn relish in place of salsa for dipping and dunking everything from nachos to celery sticks. Makes 3 quarts or 6 pint-sized jars.

6 cups fresh corn, cut off the cob
1 cup chopped onion
2 cups chopped sweet red peppers
1 cup sugar
1 tsp. salt
1 tsp. pepper
1 tsp. mustard seed
1 tsp. celery salt
2 cups cider vinegar
3 Tbsp. mustard powder
1 Tbsp. turmeric
½ cup flour
½ cup cold water

Put first 9 ingredients into kettle and mix well. Bring to boil. Lower heat and simmer for 1 hour, stirring often.

Combine mustard powder, turmeric, flour, and water in bowl and mix until smooth.

Slowly blend into corn mixture, stirring until thick. Cook until bubbles break surface for 3 minutes, stirring constantly.

Ladle into hot jars. Process pint jars 10 minutes and quart sealers 15 minutes. &

Tomatoes

By Jackie Clay

$\mathcal{I}$ wouldn't dream of calling my pantry "well-stocked" unless it had a variety of tomato products. Tomatoes can be sauced, stewed, juiced, and dried. They are easy to grow and a few well-maintained rows of prolific plants can give a family enough tomatoes to enjoy during the growing season as well as enough to preserve for the remainder of the year.

Luckily, tomatoes are one of the most versatile of garden produce. And one of the most nutritious and tasty. Besides, they are so easy to home can. They are, in fact, usually the first thing a novice home canner puts up. Here's how.

First of all, to remove the skin from tomatoes, all you have to do is get a large saucepan half full of water boiling and slide in several tomatoes, keeping the heat on. In a minute or two you can lift a tomato and see the skin split and wrinkled. It is very easy to just slip this skin off. But the tomato is very hot, so it is safest to plunge the hot tomatoes into a sink full of cold water until they cool off a bit. Then, with a paring knife, you can easily pull the skins off the tomatoes and cut out the core (stem end) by pushing the knife down around the stem and cutting out the tough whitish core.

As I've said, tomatoes are absolutely the easiest of garden produce to home can safely. And once you've had home-canned tomatoes, you'll never be satisfied with store-bought tomatoes again.

Hot-packed whole tomatoes

You can home can these large, meaty tomatoes very easily. In a large pot, I cut up some of the less perfect but juicy tomatoes and mash them down to create juice. You'll want three or four pounds. Then add your perfect, peeled, and cored tomatoes. These should be small enough to easily fit into a wide-mouthed quart or pint jar. (If your family is small, a pint will work best; if four or more, the quart will be better.)

Wash your jars and keep them in hot water. Then bring the tomatoes to a boil. I dip the hot, whole tomatoes out of the juice and pack into the jars, firmly but gently. This will create quite a bit of juice and you can add more by dipping out of your cooking pot. As there are so many low acid tomatoes out there, it's safest to add 1 Tbsp. of lemon juice to each pint and 2 Tbsp. to each quart to make sure the acidity is adequate for safe canning. You may also add 1 tsp. salt to each quart, if desired. Then fill the jar to within ½ inch of the top, removing any large air bubbles by running a small spatula or wooden spoon handle down beside the bubble to release it. (I use a chopstick.)

Wipe the rim of the jar clean and place a hot, previously simmered lid on, and screw the ring down firmly tight. Process in a hot water bath with water at least two inches over the jars. Quarts should be processed for 45 minutes and pints for 40 minutes, counting from when the boiling water in the canner *returns* to a full rolling boil after the jars have been added. Be sure there is a rack in the canner or at least a folded kitchen towel to keep the jars off the bottom of the canner. If you do not do this, some of the jar bottoms will break and you'll have tomatoes floating all around your jars.

You can also chop tomatoes and use the above instructions, or simply mash them with a potato masher while they are boiling and can, using the above instructions for tomatoes to use in a variety of other recipes.

Here's one of our favorite salsa recipes. You can experiment to get just the right amount of "heat" from the peppers.

Super salsa

20 cups peeled, cored tomatoes
10 cups chopped and seeded green bell peppers
10 cups chopped onions
2 cups chopped and seeded hot peppers (or more to taste). You can use jalapeño or
   a chili; habañero if you're brave. There is a vast difference in the hotness of
   "hot" peppers.
3-6 cloves garlic, minced
4 Tbsp. cilantro, minced
2 ½ cups white vinegar

Mix all ingredients in a large saucepan. Bring to a boil. Reduce heat, simmering 10 minutes. Dip out hot salsa into clean, hot pint jars, leaving ¼ inch of head room. Wipe jar rim clean. Place hot, previously simmered lids on jar and screw down ring firmly tight. Process in hot water bath for 15 minutes.

Removing seeds and making sauces

Now for many tomato recipes you may want to can, you'll have to remove the seeds. This is for recipes such as tomato sauce, barbecue sauce, and catsup. While you can certainly accomplish this by pressing the boiled tomatoes through a sieve or grinding them through a food mill, I much prefer using a Victorio strainer. This is a really nifty piece of kitchen gadgetry that I wouldn't want to do without. In essence, it's a food mill, like a meat grinder that crushes and presses whole, raw, skin on tomatoes (or cut large ones) through a cone-shaped screen. The juice and pulp slide down a tray into a bowl in front while you crank. And the skins and seeds drop out into another bowl from the end of the cone. No heating the tomatoes to peel them. The whole process is quick, easy, and fun, too. You can do half a bushel of tomatoes in an hour. From garden to canner. It's amazing.

To make tomato sauce, run the tomatoes through your Victorio tomato strainer or else peel, core, and heat them until they are softened, then run them through a food mill or sieve, removing all the seeds. Now you can either boil over a medium heat, stirring frequently to avoid scorching, or drain the pulp through a jelly bag if you're in a hurry. (Personally, I like the taste of the boiled sauce better, but if I'm in a hurry, through the bag it goes.) After the sauce is as thick as I want, I add just enough brown sugar to taste. If you don't, the sauce will usually taste pretty acid; this is purely a matter of taste, having nothing to do with canning.

To be safest, add a teaspoon full of lemon juice to each pint jar, then dip your sauce into the jars to can, leaving ½ inch of headroom. Process pints for 35 minutes and quarts for 40 minutes in a boiling water bath.

You can also make tomato sauce for quick use in Mexican or Italian meals by simply adjusting the spices you add. For instance, you may add basil, oregano, garlic, and minced onions, along with salt and black pepper for an Italian sauce base or chili powder, garlic, minced onions, or chipotle peppers, garlic, onions, and cilantro for a Mexican-based sauce. These are all processed for the same time as the plain tomato sauce.

Caution: Do not "tweak" these recipes by adding lots more vegetables (onions, garlic, peppers) as it could reduce the acidity of the end product, making for unsafe canning.

Spaghetti sauce

To my freshly cooked-down tomato sauce, I often add two pounds of crumbled, browned, and drained ground beef, chopped onion, chopped green and red bell peppers, oregano, basil, garlic, and sometimes mushrooms, making instant spaghetti sauce. Because this contains meat, it needs to be pressure canned, not boiling-water bathed. I simply mix all the ingredients, as though I were cooking for a fire crew, then ladle out the sauce into hot quart jars, leaving an inch of headroom. Quarts must be processed for 90 minutes at 10 pounds pressure (unless you live at an altitude of over 1,000 feet and must adjust the pressure; see your canning manual for instructions). You may process pints for 75 minutes at 10 pounds pressure.

Besides spaghetti sauce, one of our favorite tomato-based "instant" meals is chili with meat and beans. I often make a huge batch of chili on a cold winter day, then can the leftover for use in the future when I don't have so much time. Like all recipes, chili depends on your own personal taste. And even then, I make several different chili recipes, depending on what I'm feeling like that day. Here's a starter, but it's not set in stone. (You don't even need to add the beans, making a beanless chili; or leave out the meat, making a vegetarian chili.)

Chili con carne frijoles

4 lbs. ground beef or venison

2 lbs. dry beans (pintos, red kidneys or ?)

2 cups onion, chopped

1 cup green or sweet red pepper, chopped

4 tsp. salt (optional)

6 Tbsp. chili powder

2 cloves garlic, minced

2 quarts tomato sauce

6 cups chopped, peeled, cored tomatoes

2 Tbsp. brown sugar

7 ½ cups boiling water

Wash beans. Cover with cold water and soak overnight. Drain water off beans. Brown ground meat and drain off grease. Combine all ingredients and bring to boil. Boil 15 minutes. Pack hot into clean hot jars and fill liquid to within 1 inch of the top of the jar. Wipe rim of jar clean. Place hot, previously simmered lid on jar and screw down ring firmly tight. Process in pressure canner at 10 pounds (unless you live at an altitude above 1,000 feet and must adjust your pressure; see canning manual). Process pints for 75 minutes and quarts for 90 minutes.

You can home can all sorts of tomato-based recipes, from pizza sauce to Swiss steak in tomato sauce. Just multiply your recipe when you make it and be sure that if it contains meat you pressure can it.

You can also use your tomato bounty to make mincemeat, tomato preserves, your own "V-9" juice, relish, catsup, and barbecue sauces of unlimited flavors.

Tomato preserves

18 cups tomatoes, cut in chunks
6 cups sugar
3 lemons
3 tsp. ginger

Cook tomatoes 75 minutes, stirring as needed. Add sugar, thinly sliced lemon with seeds removed, and ginger. Cook until thick and smooth, then pour into sterilized pint or half-pint jars. Process in boiling water bath canner for 10 minutes.

Green tomato mincemeat

3 pints chopped, peeled tart apples
2 pints chopped green tomatoes
2 lbs. raisins
2 cups chopped suet
½ cup vinegar
4 tsp. cinnamon
2 tsp. each, salt, allspice, and cloves
6 cups sugar

Mix all ingredients and bring to a rapid boil and simmer until thick, stirring as needed to prevent scorching. Pour into clean hot jars to within 1 inch of top of jar. Wipe jar rim clean. Place hot, previously simmered lid on and screw ring down firmly tight. Process in boiling water bath for 25 minutes.

Salsa in the makings: Tomatoes, bell peppers, and chiles, right from the garden

This is virtually impossible to tell from "real" mince meat, and makes excellent mince meat pies.

V-9 juice

24 lbs. tomatoes
¾ cup each chopped carrots, celery, green pepper
¼ cup each chopped onion, parsley
bottled lemon juice

If you have a tomato strainer, simmer all vegetables until tender, then run through the mill with the tomatoes. If not, peel and core tomatoes, then quarter and simmer with vegetables until they are tender. Run through food mill or food processor, then strain to remove seeds. Stir in 1 Tbsp. salt, if desired. Add 2 Tbsp. lemon juice to each quart jar and 1 Tbsp. lemon juice to each pint jar. Fill jars to within ¼ inch of the top. Process pints 35 minutes and quarts for 40 minutes in a boiling water bath canner.

This is very good chilled. Better by far than you-know-what.

Green tomato relish chow chow

12 ½ lbs. (1 peck) green tomatoes
8 large onions
10 green or red sweet bell peppers
3 Tbsp. salt
6 seeded hot peppers
1 quart vinegar
1 ¾ cups sugar
1 Tbsp. cinnamon
1 Tbsp. allspice
¼ tsp. cloves
3 Tbsp. dry mustard

Chop tomatoes, onions, and peppers together and cover with the salt; let stand in a cool place overnight. Drain. Add the hot peppers, vinegar, and spices. Add sugar and boil slowly until tender (about 15 minutes).

Pack into hot, sterilized jars to within ½ inch of top of jar. Process in boiling water bath canner for 15 minutes (pints or half pints).

Don't tell anyone there's tomatoes in this relish and they'll ask for it at every meal!

Basic barbecue sauce

4 quarts plain tomato sauce
½ cup brown sugar
½ cup honey
6 Tbsp. Worcestershire sauce
¾ cup vinegar
1 Tbsp. dry mustard
3 tsp. salt

Combine all ingredients and simmer 15 minutes until as thick as desired. Ladle into hot, sterilized pint jars and process 20 minutes in a boiling water bath. You can personalize this recipe to taste. For a sweeter sauce, add more brown sugar. For a nifty, spicy sauce, add a few dried chipolte peppers in a spice bag to the simmering sauce. The variations are simply unlimited. Just be sure to process it for 20 minutes.

Tomato catsup

22 lbs. (1 peck) ripe tomatoes
2 medium onions
2 cups vinegar
½ cup sweet red pepper
1½ tsp. celery seed
1 tsp. whole allspice
1 tsp. mustard seed
1 stick cinnamon
1 cup sugar
1 Tbsp. salt
1 Tbsp. paprika

Combine peeled, cored, quartered tomatoes with onion and pepper in large saucepan, cooking until tender. Run through food mill or tomato mill. Cook down until reduced by one half, stirring often to prevent scorching. Tie spices in spice bag. Add spice bag, sugar, salt, and paprika to tomato mixture. Simmer 25 minutes, stirring frequently. Remove spice bag. Ladle hot catsup into hot pint jars, leaving ¼ inch headroom. Process 10 minutes in a boiling water bath. If you live at an altitude above 1,000 feet, consult your canning manual to adjust processing time as necessary.

Green tomato apple pie and fried green tomatoes

And talking about recipes for tomatoes, I would be remiss not to mention green tomato apple pie. This great recipe uses those little hard tomatoes that are left after you pick all you can in the fall, when frost threatens. Or any time you feel like it. Simply use hard, very green tomatoes, and core and slice them like apples. You don't need to peel them. Then use them in your favorite apple pie recipe. You truly can't tell it from apple. This way you can have homemade apple pie while your orchard is still too young to bear.

Then, there is fried green tomatoes. You just slice a meaty, whole large green tomato into quarter-inch-thick slices and dip them into a mixture of flour, cornmeal, salt, and pepper. Then fry them on each side until they are golden and tasty. Eat 'em hot. Mmmmm.

Dried tomatoes

Tomatoes are very easy to dry. I pick the nice ripe, large, meaty cherry-paste tomatoes such as Principe Borghese or a Roma type. You want more meat than juice, as a real juicy tomato is harder to get dry before it molds.

To dry small, meaty tomatoes, simply slice them in half and remove the stem and core, if necessary. Place on a single layer on your dehydrator tray and dry until they are nearly stiff and leathery. You can dry them on cookie sheets, but they must be turned as they dry to prevent them from sticking ferociously to the pan. They can also be dried on cookie sheets or screens in your gas oven with only the pilot light on for heat.

Once dried, the leathery tomatoes can be stored nearly indefinitely in airtight glass jars. Watch the jars carefully for the first week. At the first sign of any sweating or condensation on the sides of the jar, remove the tomatoes and dry some more or they will mold.

You can add a bit of boiling water to the tomatoes in a dish to reconstitute, or add to olive oil. They are great on pizza or in any tomato dish. We like to snack on these great treats. Our favorites are dried Sungold halves. This golden cherry tomato is so sweet that the dried halves taste like dried apricots.

Okay, you've enjoyed your tomatoes all summer and fall. The vines are still giving you a harvest, albeit not as heavy as before and are getting tired. But all of a sudden, the weather turns clear and nippy at night and you hear the dreaded "F" word on the weather radio. The first few light frosts can be headed off by covering the plants with tarps, plastic sheets, or even bedding.

But sooner or later, the end is near and a freeze warning comes. It will be too cold to protect the plants. So gather every tomato you want to save. Separate them by stages of ripeness: Red, yellow, yellow-green, and dark green. The red ones, you can put up soon. The yellow and yellow-green tomatoes will sit happily in buckets, boxes, and baskets for a week or two until they happily ripen for your next go-around. My son, David, grew up with his bottom bunk littered with various containers of ripening tomatoes each fall.

Even the large green tomatoes will usually ripen well, unwrapped, just sitting in a warm place. Don't put them on a sunny window sill; they will often rot, rather than ripen.

The little dark green tomatoes probably won't ripen, so use them for your green apple pies, mince meat, dill green tomatoes, relishes, and whatever else you decide you'd like to try. They are really very useful, so don't simply toss them or let them freeze. (Once tomatoes are touched by a bad frost or frozen, they will usually quickly rot.) 🍂

Drying, Smoking, and Pickling Foods

"Our life is frittered away by detail. Simplify, simplify."

Henry David Thoreau

Alternative methods for food preservation

By Jackie Clay

When one is striving for a self-reliant lifestyle, food is one of the most important things to consider. "Grow your own!" is our battle cry. Our garden is bountiful and we spend a blissful summer, eating chiefly from it: fresh beans, squash, corn, cukes, lettuce, chard, broccoli, and more. And of course, we butcher our home-raised chickens and pig, harvest our deer in the fall, and enjoy fresh rolls from our homegrown wheat.

We certainly can up tons and tons of great food to serve not only during the winter, but during the coming years, as well. But have you considered the other methods of food preservation? Like canning, there are several other tried and true ways to put up your bounty. (If you've read any pioneering books, like Laura Ingalls Wilder's series of *Little House* books, you'll remember some of them.)

Not only do the other methods of preserving food give you an alternate way of keeping food from spoiling, but more importantly, I think, they provide variety and interest to your everyday meals.

There are a few alternative food preservation methods I'm not going into detail about. These include salting and larding. Both of these methods *do* keep food, but due to health concerns, they probably aren't a great idea today. We are all trying valiantly to cut down on our salt intake to improve our blood pressure and also to reduce our fat consumption so our heart lasts as long as our plans and dreams do. I'll also skip over freezing. Yes, you can freeze most foods, but if you lose power, there goes your food. Or the freezer quietly dies and you lose your food without even knowing you've got a problem. Or the food stays in the freezer too long and develops freezer burn. Instead, here are some other methods you might want to try.

Dehydration

Dehydrating food at home is a great idea. The food remains very fresh-tasting on rehydration, it takes very little room to store, the food is extremely light so it can be carried, and best of all, dehydrating is very easy and fun to do. Like canning, once you start, you will be on a mission.

Is it hard? Expensive to get into? No to both questions. If you can cut up food, you can dehydrate it. There are no "sulfuring" or lengthy pre-treatments necessary. And you can pick up a new electric dehydrator for less than $50 at most stores that carry canning equipment. I got mine several years back from Wal-Mart. My second one came from our local thrift store, complete with fruit leather trays and a manual for $3.

I've also dehydrated on nylon window screens in the back of our sun-heated Suburban with the window up, on flat roof tops, the hot, dry attic, and in the oven of my gas range with only the pilot on. Dehydrating is an ancient art, requiring no special equipment. But I will say that using an electric dehydrator sure makes things easier, quicker, and more reliable.

We live far off grid, but use the dehydrator when we have the generator on for a few hours for my writing or tool use. It's a little peculiar, but it works.

Here are instructions for dehydrating several foods so you'll get the idea. Then pick up a good book—even at the library if you can't afford to buy one—and read it thoroughly, making notes for the future. Like I said, dehydrating is really easy for anyone to do. The main things are to lay the food out in a single layer so the pieces don't overlap, and to check the trays periodically to make sure one area isn't drying faster than the others. You may need to switch trays around to ensure that the food dries evenly throughout the entire dehydrator. Make *sure* the food is dried to the dryness recommended for each food. If there is too much moisture in the food, it will mold. You will be storing your dehydrated food in airtight containers, probably jars. Pay special attention right after you store the newly dehydrated pieces. If there is any condensation on the inside of the jars, *immediately* put the pieces back in the dehydrator and dry a little longer.

Home dehydrating is easy and the food tastes good. An added bonus is that a bushel of produce can be dehydrated and stored in a couple of jars. Many foods contain up to 90 percent water. Pick up a good book on dehydrating food, and go at it.

Peas:

Peas are very easy to dehydrate at home. Simply shell your peas, then dip them into boiling water for one minute to blanch them. If you don't, the flavor will not keep as well. Let them drip dry, then spread them out on your trays, one layer deep. Dehydrate until they are hard and puckered. If using a cookie sheet, stir them a time or two.

Cool and pour into airtight, vermin-proof containers. I use odd shaped glass jars. I keep at least two gallons in storage, and they'll last for years. Rehydrate in boiling water and let them steep for an hour or two. For use in soups and stews, simply sprinkle a handful or two of dried peas into your stock. Simmer until done. Simple and tasty.

Not enough peas in the garden to dehydrate? Buy some on-sale frozen peas, thaw 'em, and go at it. They work fine.

Onions and garlic:

Onions and garlic are about as easy as it gets. I peel them and slice whole round slices off, about an eighth of an inch thick. Place in a single layer on your tray and begin dehydrating. Dry until quite dry. I then chop them, either using a blender (when the generator is on) or in a food grinder. Dump the chopped onions out on a cookie sheet and dry further, until crunchy-dry. These may be stored as is or reduced to a textured powder to use in cooking as onion powder. I do some of each, and keep a quart of onion powder, a half pint of garlic powder, a quart of minced onion, and a half pint of minced garlic on my pantry shelf. I use these every day.

Corn:

Sweet corn is another of my favorites. I briefly boil a couple dozen ears of corn, then cut the kernels off the cob and lay them on a drying tray in a single layer. Corn needs to be stirred often if on a cookie sheet, but is fine on a screen or regular dehydrator tray. Dry until tough and hard, then store in an airtight jar or other container. To rehydrate and use as fresh corn, I boil it for one minute, then place in the fridge overnight. The next day it's hard to tell from fresh corn. This sweet corn will keep for years in decent storage. If you run out of fresh corn, frozen or canned corn will dehydrate fine.

Carrots:

Carrots dehydrate great at home. Slice or dice the carrots into ¼-inch pieces. Blanch for one minute in steam or boiling water. Drip dry and put on a tray in a single layer. Dehydrate until leathery and quite hard.

String beans:

Use any variety with small seeds, yellow or green. Wash, string if necessary, cut off ends, and cut into 1-inch pieces. Blanch for 4-6 minutes, drain. Dry until brittle. Rehydrate before use. In the old days, folks used to use a needle and strong thread and string whole green beans and hang them from the rafters until dry. These are called leather britches and are very good. Like the apples, you do run a risk of having them pick up a little dust, but you can rinse before rehydrating in boiling water. They have a flavor of their own that many older people fondly remember from their childhood.

Peppers:

Peppers of all kinds dehydrate wonderfully. The old way was to string them by the stems and hang in the sun on a porch wall. But if you live in a humid climate, you'll probably have molded peppers if you use this method. So use the dehydrator method. Seed the peppers, then halve thin-walled hot peppers or slice thick-walled peppers, such as bell peppers, in ¼-inch wide slices. Dehydrate in a single layer until crunchy.

Broccoli:

Broccoli works great dehydrated, which is lucky because it is terrible when canned. Cut into small flowerettes and blanch. Lay out in a single layer and dehydrate to a very crisp texture, like artificial little trees. It works great in cheese and broccoli soup and casseroles.

Mushrooms:

Wash gently to remove dirt, but don't soak in water. Cut into ¼-inch slices. Dry until brittle. Use in stews, soups, on pizzas, or in casseroles.

Hot peppers:

Rinse, cut into pieces about ½ inch thick or halve small chiles. You may also roast the peppers on a grill or in your oven until the skins are charred, place in a paper bag for an hour or so, then dip in ice water to remove skins. Then dehydrate. Peppers should be crisp when dehydrated. You may also whir in a blender to make your own hot seasoning powder.

Sweet peppers:

Wash, remove stems and seeds. Slice or dice in ½-inch pieces. Dry until leathery/brittle. Use in stews, on pizzas, in casseroles, Spanish rice, or for general seasoning.

Tomatoes:

Use a meaty type tomato that isn't too juicy. Wash, dip in boiling water for 30 seconds, then hold in cold water. Remove skins. Core if necessary. Cut into ¼ to ½-inch slices. Dry until crisp. You can also sprinkle moist tomato slices with Italian seasonings such as basil or oregano. We like dehydrated Sungold cherry tomatoes as a snack. They are very fruity and sweet, almost like apricots. You can use dehydrated tomatoes in soups, stews, on pizzas, or in general cooking. You can also powder in a blender for an even more versatile product. Like the onion powder, return the tomato powder to the dehydrator trays, lined with fruit leather plastic trays, and dehydrate more to be sure no moisture remains that would cause clumping during storage.

Potatoes:

Wash, peel, and cut into ¼-inch slices. Blanch for 5-6 minutes. Rinse well in cold water, which removes starch that would make them less palatable. Dry until brittle. Use in potatoes au gratin, scalloped potatoes, stews, and other combined dishes. You can also grate the potatoes with a coarse grater, blanch, rinse and pat dry, and use these as dehydrated hash browns.

Pumpkin:

Pumpkin and winter squash are dehydrated the same way. Peel and remove seeds and goop. Cut into ¼-inch strips. Blanch for 2 minutes, then drain and dry until brittle. Use in baking, soups, and stews. Like the leather britches above, homesteaders and Native Americans in days past used to string up or hang rings of pumpkin and squash on small poles to dry in hot autumn days. I often toss a handful of dried pumpkin or squash into the blender and grind it—then add it to my multigrain bread. You never know it's there, but there *is* a decidedly good sweetness and taste you can't put your finger on. (Of course you don't tell anyone you put squash in the bread!)

Fruits are simple to dehydrate, too. You can just slice ripe **bananas** ¼-inch thick onto your tray and dry them to a leathery-hard disc. **Peach** slices are equally easy. Make your own raisins from whole seedless **grapes**. Just stem them, sort and lay out in a single layer. Easy? You bet.

Apples:

Peel, core, and slice solid apples into ½-inch thick slices or rings. To keep from turning brown, soak the slices in 1 cup lemon juice to 1 quart of water for 10 minutes or in 1 Tbsp. ascorbic acid (Vitamin C tablets, crushed) in 1 quart of water. Neither will affect the taste of the apples and they will keep white. Lay on a single layer on your dehydrator trays and dry until they are leathery. In the old days, apple rings were strung on stout string and hung from the rafters of the hot attic to dry. While this works well today, you do risk having dust and insects on the drying apples. Use as a snack or in pies, crisps, and other baked goods. You can also make sweet spiced apple pieces by rolling the pieces in cinnamon sugar before dehydrating. They are very good.

A bowl of fresh strawberries waiting to be dehydrated

Cherries:

Wash, cut in half, and pit. Lay in a single layer on your dehydrator trays and dehydrate until leathery and slightly sticky like raisins.

Seedless grapes and blueberries:

Wash and stem fruit. Dip into boiling water for 30 seconds to crack skin. This lets them dry "wrinkled" instead of "fat" looking, which isn't too appealing. Dry until leathery as raisins. Use as a snack or in baked goods.

Raspberries or blackberries:

Simply pick through the berries, removing any stems or leaves. Lay in a single layer and dry until leathery. Quick and tasty.

Pineapple:

Peel, core, and slice fully ripe pineapple. Cut into ½-inch slices. You may roll the pieces in sugar to dehydrate "sugared" pineapple, like you get in trail mixes, or simply dehydrate for a natural fruit. Use as a snack or in baked goods.

Strawberries:

Remove the leaves and core of fully ripe strawberries. Cut smaller berries into halves or larger ones into ½-inch slices. Dry until more crisp than leathery. You can also grind the dehydrated slices for ease of using in yogurt, desserts, and baked goods. They don't rehydrate well; the color is darkened and they look unappetizing.

Peaches:
Peel by immersing in boiling water for a minute, then remove pit. Cut into ½-inch slices and dip into either lemon water or ascorbic acid water to keep from darkening. Dry until leathery. Use as a snack or in baked goods and desserts.

Fruit leathers:
You can make fruit leather out of just about any fruit or combination that appeals to you. I often do apple/raspberry or strawberry. It makes the berries go further, as we are often short of wild berries. To make the fruit leather, rinse the fruit, remove the pits/seeds. Puree in a blender until smooth or run through a food mill. Add any sweetener or spices you want. Mix well. Cover dehydrator trays with a heavy food grade plastic wrap or use the special fruit leather sheets that come with your dehydrator. Spread puree evenly ^{1}/8 inch thick on trays. Dry until it is pliable, yet leathery. Peel up and check for moisture. Roll up like a jelly roll and cut into convenient pieces.

Jerky:
Besides dehydrating fruits and vegetables, you can dehydrate meat of all kinds. Do *not* try to dehydrate meat with fat on it, because it will get rancid during storage. Use only lean meat. If you want to make jerky out of hamburger, choose only the extra lean or else be sure to freeze or refrigerate while you wait to use it.

To dehydrate meat and poultry, debone it and cut off all fat and gristle. Slice into pieces ¼ inch thick, across the grain to get the most tender cuts. You may marinate it overnight in the refrigerator in your favorite recipe. This does not affect the keeping quality of the product, only the taste. Typical marinades include vinegar, brown sugar, soy sauce, Italian dressing, etc.

Drain your meat/poultry pieces, then lay out on your dehydrator trays. I always use a fruit leather tray on the bottom to catch the inevitable drips and make cleanup easier. Meat that is dehydrated must be brought up to a temperature of 160° F if it is going to be stored on the shelf. You can do this by boiling it in the marinade for five minutes before dehydrating or by putting the dehydrated meat in the oven and baking at 275° F for 10 minutes.

Meat should be dehydrated until it is very leathery. The drier the better. If it has any moisture, it will cause condensation on the inside of storage jars and will mold. Check it very closely the first few days. If you see *any* condensation, redo it for a few hours more.

In the old days, jerky and dried meat was dried to a stick-like consistency. It had to be held in the mouth several minutes before you could even begin to chew it. Today's jerky is usually softer for ease of eating, but commercial jerky also has preservatives in it to keep it from spoiling; your homemade dry meat either needs to be refrigerated if you want it a bit softer or dried *very dry* to keep on the shelf.

Rehydrating dried foods

Some of your dehydrated food can be used as is, when used in soups, stews, or other moist dishes. Vegetables, especially, can just be tossed in boiling water like you would do to cook fresh ones. They'll rehydrate quickly and plump up nicely. I rehydrate my string beans and potato slices before use; they are more tender and will cook more dependably that way. Simply pour boiling water over them and wait until they are plump. So simple!

You can also rehydrate fruit to use as a dessert or in baked recipes. Simply pour boiling water over the dry fruit and let set until it is plumped up. It will take about 10 minutes. Drain and add sugar or honey, if desired.

Smoking meat

Smoking meat is an ancient food preservation method. While it does make meat last a long while, it is only safely effective during the cold months. High temperatures are hard on smoked meat and even properly cured meat will spoil after awhile. Smoked meat has a sweet, unique flavor and a smokehouse full of home-cured bacon, ham, shoulder, venison, and fish makes winter a wonderful time of the year. Absolutely nothing smells better than entering a cold smokehouse or other meat storage pantry and savoring the aroma about you.

Is smoking meat difficult? No, but it does take a little trial and error to get it perfect. You *can* get edible, good-flavored meat on your very first attempt. But like all homestead skills, practice makes perfect. My first smoking experience was with fish. They are easy to start with because they are smaller and easier to quickly smoke. A neighbor brought me a pan of home-smoked suckers. Not wanting to be impolite, I gingerly nibbled on a bit of one offered to me. *Wow!* I really, really liked it. Suckers are "trash" fish and ugly to boot, but they instantly took on a whole different aura.

With the neighbor's help, I turned an old junk clothes dryer into a sucker smoker. Basically, we just took out the drum, turning the dryer into a "closet" of sorts. I mounted two old broomsticks across the top of it and I was in business. To make the smoke needed, I simply used a small electric hotplate scavenged from the dump and an old cast iron frying pan full of apple wood chips. Turned on low, the hotplate burned the wood chips, creating a nice cool, dense smoke. I only had to add chips a few times during the day and night, and I had the perfect smoking fire.

Soon after, we caught our own bunch of suckers out of the nearby creek where they were going to spawn. After gutting them, I cut off the heads and soaked them overnight in a mild brine made of 1 cup non-iodized salt to 1 gallon of cold water, with ½ cup brown sugar added. Then I held the fish open with small sharpened branches and hung them from the broomsticks by heavy strings run through the meat just below the bone behind the gill area. No fish were close enough to touch. The spring days were cool and the nights cooler—the perfect weather for cold smoking. I turned on my hot plate and shut the door. The smoker should not get hotter than 70° F during the smoking process for fish.

Smoke medium-large fish all day and night if you plan on eating the fish soon or freezing or canning them after smoking. If you plan on keeping them longer, they must be held in the operating smoker for up to a week. This turns the fish leathery, driving out all moisture. During the long smoking period, you have to man the fire 24/7 or the smoking is ineffective. I smoke my fish for 24 hours, then can it. This works very well for me.

When you say "smoked meat," bacon and ham instantly come to mind. Of course, venison and beef may be smoked in the same way. In smoking meat, as with smoking fish, there are actually two steps, the cure and the actual smoking. The cure serves to help tenderize the meat and protect it from spoilage during the smoking.

There are two basic types of cures, the brine cure that I used for my fish and the dry cure. While I like the brine cure for fish, as it kind of draws out any "fishy" taste, the dry cure generally works best for meat. It is also easier for the beginner to use.

You can buy prepackaged mixtures for your dry cure from many local stores that sell hunting supplies, or from your meat market. There are also many mail order supply houses that sell cures. Many cures contain saltpeter. This controversial ingredient is believed by some to be a carcinogen, but it has been used—and is still used commercially—for generations in meat cures. It keeps the attractive reddish color of the finished smoked meat. Personally, I prefer not to use it. My meat is darker in color and maybe not as beautiful, but I feel better having left it out. Saltpeter does nothing to keep the meat from spoiling.

One homemade cure formula for 100 pounds of meat is 8 pounds pickling salt and 2 pounds of brown sugar, mixed well. If you choose to add the saltpeter, you would add 2 ounces also. Keep your meat between 38 and 40° F before curing, then try to hold it around that temperature during curing.

You will use about 1 ounce of the dry cure per pound of ham and a bit less per pound of bacon. Rub it well into the meat to be cured. For larger pieces of meat, ham for instance, you will rub ^{1}/3 of the amount, three times, then again a week after the last treatment. Hang the meat so it can drip into a pan below, not onto meat held on lower shelves. You'll cure a side of bacon in 14 days or a ham in a little over a month. Remember to keep the meat around 40° F for safest curing. When the cure is complete, it's time to smoke.

You can build a smokehouse if you are really serious about smoking quantities of meat each year. A smokehouse is simply a small building the size of a small outhouse, usually built of block, that is varmint-proof and convenient to work in. You can find plans in many books. You can even make a "smokehouse" out of a barrel with a fire pit located in the ground a few feet away and a buried stovepipe leading from it, upward to the bottom of the barrel that contains your meat. The main thing is to contain much of the smoke, yet not raise the temperature of the smoke-house higher than 90 ° F. This is a "cool" smoke and does more to pre-serve the meat than a hot smoke does.

Run a strong cord through your meat so it can hang from poles at the top of your smokehouse. There should be enough room so that the meat pieces do not touch. This lets the smoke completely surround and pen-etrate the meat. To keep the meat from becoming too salty, you can scrub the outside of the cured meat with fresh water and a brush, then dry it overnight before you smoke it.

The type of wood you choose for smoking greatly affects the taste of your finished product. Some good woods are maple, apple, cherry, mesquite, and alder. Do *not* use pine or any other evergreen. The meat will end up nearly inedible.

The larger the meat pieces are, the longer they need to smoke. In gen-eral, bacon will usually be adequately smoked in a 24 hour period or a little longer. You want the outside golden brown, not dark saddle brown. Hams and shoulders usually will be adequately smoked in about 48 hours or a little longer. In the old days, folks smoked their meat longer, resulting in a more jerky-like end product. It held well for long periods but was not as tender as most people like today. Cured, smoked meat will keep all winter and into the spring. But as the days get hot, the meat can become bug infested and spoil.

For this reason, I usually use up most of my smoked meat during the winter and can up the rest for later use. Once in the jar, it is good for many, many years.

Pickling

When you say "pickling," most people think dill or sweet pickles or other cucumber products. But pickling has a much broader scope. You can also pickle onions, carrots, beans, cauliflower, peppers, cabbage, mushrooms, eggs, fish, and meat. While you probably wouldn't sit down to a meal of pickled this or that, pickling definitely has a place on the homestead, as it is a reliable way not only to preserve more food, but to preserve it in a way that gives it a unique flavor. This does a lot to relieve boredom, especially when times are less than wonderful. Often when you eat well, you feel well too.

Here is a sampling of great pickling recipes. If you want more, check your interlibrary loan or Amazon.com for the wonderful pickling book, *The Complete Book of Pickles and Relishes* by Leonard Lewis Levinson. It's out of print, but it's one of my very favorites.

Mustard beans:
(Tastes like honey mustard sauce, not "mustardy" at all.)

8 quarts green or wax beans
salt
6 cups sugar
1 cup flour
5 Tbsp. dry mustard powder
1 Tbsp. turmeric
6 cups vinegar

Simmer beans, cut into 1-inch pieces if desired, in salted water until barely tender. You do not want to "cook" them; they are pickles. Drain.

115

Mix dry ingredients in large saucepan. Add vinegar and bring to a boil. Stir well. Add drained beans and bring to a boil. Simmer 5 minutes. Pack into hot sterilized jars. Process in a water bath canner for 10 minutes.

Pickled onions:

1 gallon small onions
1 cup salt
2 cups sugar
6 cups white vinegar

Scald onions for 2 minutes in boiling water. Dip out and hold in cold water. Peel. Sprinkle with salt. Add ice water and let stand overnight. Drain. Rinse. Drain again.

Add sugar to vinegar. Simmer 10 minutes. Pack onions into hot sterilized jars. Heat pickling liquid to boiling. Ladle over onions to within ½ inch of the top of the jar. Process in water bath canner for 10 minutes.

Pickled peppers:

1 gallon peppers
1½ cups pickling salt
1 gallon ice water
5 cups vinegar
1 cup sugar

Wash and drain long Hungarian or other peppers. Cut 2 small slits in each pepper or cut in half, removing the seeds. Dissolve salt in 1 gallon ice water and pour over peppers in a large roasting pan. Let stand overnight. Drain, rinse, and drain again.

Add sugar to vinegar. Simmer 15 minutes. Pack peppers into hot, sterilized jars. Heat pickling liquid to boiling and pour over peppers to ½ inch of top of jar. Process for 15 minutes in boiling water bath.

I use these peppers, sliced, on my pizzas. Very good.

Pickled eggs:

20 eggs
2 cups white vinegar
1½ quarts water
2 tsp. salt
1 small dry hot pepper
1 Tbsp. mixed pickling spices

Simmer eggs for 30 minutes to make hardboiled eggs. Cool in cold water and peel.

Make a pickling solution of the remaining ingredients, adding spices in a spice bag. Bring to a boil. Add peeled eggs and bring to a boil again. Pack into hot, sterilized jars. Ladle hot pickling solution over the eggs, completely covering them, to within 1 inch of the top of the jar. Process for 10 minutes in a boiling water bath.

Corned beef:

8 qts. cold water
3 lbs. pickling salt
2 Tbsp. brown sugar
1 oz. sodium nitrate (optional; saves red color in meat)
1 Tbsp. mixed pickling spices
20 bay leaves
10 lbs. lean beef brisket
8 cloves of garlic

Combine all ingredients except meat and simmer for 10 minutes. Place meat in a crock with a tight fitting cover. Add garlic, pour cold pickling solution over meat. Weight meat down with a heavy plate and sterilized rock (boiled). Put on crock cover and cover that with 2 layers of clean cloth, tied tightly around crock. Store in a cool (38-40° F) place for 2 weeks. Use after that time or can chunks up.

Pickled mixed vegetables:

2 heads cauliflower
1 quart peeled carrots
1½ cups small whole peeled onions
¼ cup salt
2½ cups sugar
2 Tbsp. mustard seed
1 Tbsp. celery seed
1 tsp. turmeric
2 qt. white vinegar
1 hot dry red pepper (optional)

Cut cauliflower into smaller pieces. Cut carrots into slices or smaller chunks. Add onions and sprinkle salt over them and cover with ice water. Let stand for 3 hours. Drain, rinse, and drain again. In a large saucepan, combine sugar, spices, and vinegar. If you want hot pickled veggies, add hot pepper to vinegar mix. Bring to a boil. Add flowerets, onions, and carrots and bring to a boil again. Boil until vegetables are just barely tender. Pack hot vegetables into hot jar and ladle pickling solution to cover them to within ½ inch of the top of the jar. Process in a hot water bath for 10 minutes.

As you can readily see, you can sure pickle a wide assortment of foods that give variety to your pantry. This is one good reason to use all these alternative methods of putting up food; you get a great variety of tongue tingling tastes at every meal. Boring meals are not acceptable. We can do much better when we combine our traditional home canning with dehydrated, smoked, and pickled foods too. Toss in a few jams, jellies, and preserves along with breads and rolls from our homegrown grains and every single meal is a celebration of self-reliant living. You can't get that satisfied feeling by dumping something out of a box. 🌺

Jerky

By Linda Gabris

Nothing makes a better snack than a chewy, spicy stick of mouth-watering jerky. No matter how much of the delicious leathery stuff I make, it's never enough. A staple food of aboriginal people, mountain men, and settlers, today jerky is considered a delicacy which sells at hefty dollars a pound.

The term "jerky" comes from Quechuan Indians of Peru. It refers to their method of putting up fresh kill by drying meat in the sun. One of the oldest and simplest forms of meat preservation, jerking allows the meat to be stored indefinitely.

Jerked meat, or jerky, is one of the best ways I know of saving ill-fated game or other meat in the freezer that's about to expire its prime shelf life. And it's a great way to rid the fridge of a build-up of less desirable cuts.

It is easy to personalize jerky to suit any taste. It can be hot and spicy, sweet and mild, brittle, or leathery, whatever tickles your fancy.

Unlike earlier cultures that relied on sun for drying, folks today can dry meat by various methods including conventional oven, food dehydrator, or smoker. If you have a dehydrator or smoker, no doubt you already have instructions in your manual on how to make jerky using these devices. So for those just starting out in the world of jerked meat, here's a basic method for making a delicious batch of jerky in your range oven.

Once you've got a taste for jerky, you might want to buy a portable electric smoker or build an old-fashioned smokehouse to pursue your

*Slicing a moose chuck roast
into thin strips for jerky*

new hobby, as nothing beats the exotic flavor of real smoke derived from maple, cherry, hickory, or other fragrant wood chips.

Commercial jerky is usually made out of beef, but I've found that venison meats including deer, moose, elk, and caribou make a superior stick. A haunch of deer or lower shoulder of bigger animal like moose is ideal for making into jerky, but any cuts will do as long as you can strip the meat thinly. If using fresh meat, partially freeze it to enable easier handling and more uniform slices. If meat is previously frozen, thaw enough to slice.

One of the tricks to great jerky is in the marinade. A rich spicy marinade will produce full-flavored jerky. When selecting liquid and spice make sure they will instill flavors and aroma that you'll enjoy. You can be creative when mixing marinade and customize as you wish by increasing or omitting any seasoning or adding spice and herbs of your choice.

Wine adds flavor and contains acid that helps breaks down fiber, but diluted or herbed vinegar can be used in place. The longer the meat is submerged, the more infused it will be.

Jerked meat is approximately ¼ the weight of its fresh state, so from four pounds of meat you'll end up with about a pound of jerky making it understandable why it's so expensive in stores.

Oven-easy venison jerky

4 lbs. lean boneless venison

Marinade:
1 cup red wine
¾ cup soy sauce
shake of Worcestershire sauce
¼ cup maple syrup (or liquid honey)
2 ounces liquid smoke
3 tsp. salt
3 tsp. garlic powder
2 tsp. onion powder
2 tsp. fresh ground black pepper
pinch of crushed chilies or cayenne, if you like it hot

Mix the marinade ingredients in large glass or stainless steel bowl. Using a sharp knife, cut the meat into strips as long and uniformly thin (about 3/8-inch thick) as possible, bearing in mind that the thinner the meat, the quicker the drying time and the more brittle the jerky will be. For leathery jerky, leave a little thicker. When all the meat is stripped, lay each piece on a board and pound it gently with a mallet to break tissue, then place in marinade. Let marinate under refrigeration for at least eight hours.

Ready to dry

Line oven with foil to collect drippings and put cloth or paper under door to catch condensation. Spray racks with non-stick coating. Shake excess marinade from meat and place on racks making sure pieces do not touch. Preheat oven to 150° F. Put in racks and let meat dry 15 minutes leaving door ajar so steam can escape. Reduce heat to 120° F and allow meat to dry for six hours then turn strips over and continue drying for another two or three hours or until desired dryness is reached.

Storing

After jerky has cooled, remove from racks and place in air-tight containers. Store in cool, dry place. Although it is said that jerky keeps forever, I doubt this has ever been proven as it's so good who could resist temptation that long.

Modern day pemmican

When I'm on the trail, I like food that's fast and filling, and what could be easier than a lunch that's scooped up and eaten with the fingers in traditional fashion. Once you've got jerky, you can make pemmican which is a highly nutritious, super energy food that was a popular staple of North American Indian people.

To make this interesting concoction, jerked meat is pounded with a hammer into powder and mixed with an equal amount of fat and then spiked with dried wild fruit or berries. Aboriginal people used rendered fish grease or bear fat, but I have found that the most pleasant-tasting and healthiest choice of 'fat' for modern-day pemmican is peanut butter.

½ cup jerked meat powder

½ cup chunky peanut butter

1 cup chopped mixed dried fruit, seeds, nuts (currents, apples, dates, figs, cranberries, almonds, sesame...)

pinch nutmeg or other spice of choice

Mix ingredients thoroughly. Indians packed their pemmican into leather pouches but a little jar or crock does fine. Pemmican saves for months without refrigeration making it an ideal backpacking food. Spread it on rye bread for a perfect trail lunch.

Great home-cooked meals from your storage pantry

By Jackie Clay

For some reason, cooking from a long-term storage pantry makes many people cringe. Maybe they are envisioning endless meals of boiled beans and plain piles of white rice. You know, "survival" food.

We eat out of our pantry, three meals a day, seven days a week, at least to some extent. And we aren't forcing down unpalatable food, just to "rotate" our foods, either. I'm no gourmet cook, but visitors tend to sniff the air when coming into our house. "Mmmm...what's that?" We answer, somewhat smugly, I'll admit, and laughingly set another plate or two at the table.

Eating out of a pantry is not just something you do during an emergency. It is a tasty, very economical way of meal planning. But don't you have to spend hours cooking meals from the pantry? Hardly. A lot of

With a good storage pantry you can eat well all of the time.

days, I don't have fifteen minutes to cook a meal and the storage pantry is a real lifesaver. (We live an hour and a half from a fast food restaurant, so we can't just run to Mickie D's for a takeout when we're busy.)

So, to better acquaint you with just what can be done with storage foods, I've picked out a few of our favorites. They are very flexible; if you have fresh or homecanned veggies, you can substitute those for reconstituted dehydrated vegetables. Or if you have fresh meat, you can substitute it for homecanned. You get the picture.

Casseroles

Casseroles of all types are among the most versatile ways to use our pantry foods. They stick to your ribs, are fast and easy to put together, and make good use of a wide variety of foods from our pantry shelves. Here are a few of our favorites.

Cheesie vegetable casserole

In a two quart casserole dish, layer the following, in this order:

3 large potatoes, peeled and sliced, or 1½ cups dehydrated potatoes, reconstituted in 1 cup of boiling water until nearly tender, or 1 pint sliced, home canned potatoes without liquid

1 pint sweet corn or 1 cup dehydrated corn reconstituted the day before in 2 cups boiling water and set overnight in fridge

1 pint carrots or 1 cup dehydrated carrots, reconstituted the day before in 2 cups boiling water and set overnight in fridge

½ cup cheddar cheese powder

½ cup dehydrated milk

dehydrated onions

grated cheese

Mix ½ cup of cheddar cheese powder and ½ cup of dehydrated milk with enough warm water to cover vegetables slightly. Sprinkle top with dehydrated sliced onions. Bake at 350° F until almost done, then sprinkle top with grated cheese and finish baking until cheese is melted and bubbly.

This casserole is flexible; you can vary the vegetables as you want or need to, or you can add any leftover pieces of boneless meat or poultry. We use it often and never get tired of it. It's especially good with home baked whole wheat rolls.

Chicken noodle bake

3 cups dry wide noodles or homemade noodles

2 Tbsp. margarine

1 onion, sliced or 1 Tbsp. dehydrated

1 pint boneless chicken breast

1 tsp. black pepper

2 cups milk (dry or fresh)

2 Tbsp. flour

half pint mushrooms or a quarter cup dehydrated and rehydrated in boiling water

1 cup coarse bread crumbs

1 tsp. salt

1 tsp. ground sage

3 Tbsp. margarine

In a large saucepan, simmer noodles in water until tender.

Meanwhile in a medium saucepan, over medium heat, melt the margarine. Then saute onion and mushrooms in it until slightly browned. Add flour while stirring. Add 2 cups of milk and stir over heat until beginning to thicken. Quickly add salt, pepper, and sage and stir in well. Add more milk, if needed to make a medium sauce, a bit on the thin side. Stir in drained noodles and stir gently. Then add sliced, boneless, skinless chicken and stir once again, gently.

Slide mixture into a casserole dish and pat down evenly. Sprinkle with coarse bread crumbs and drizzle with melted margarine. (You can add a layer of half mushrooms, stuffed with minced chicken, mixed with creamed cheese and a pinch of dehydrated onion for special occasions! Then add bread crumbs and melted margarine.) Bake at 350° F until done.

Again, this recipe is versatile; you can add vegetables, double the recipe for larger gatherings, or "fancy" it up with the chicken-creamed cheese stuffed mushrooms (our favorite is wild morels), stuffed jalapeños, or even carrot curls.

Chili cheese bake

1 quart of home-canned chili with beans (To make a quart of chili for this recipe I use 1 cup dry pinto or red kidney beans soaked overnight and simmered the next day to tender, ½ pound fried, crumbled hamburger with 1 chopped onion (or dehydrated equivalent), one pint of tomato sauce or chopped tomatoes, ½ tsp. cumin, 1 tsp. salt, 1 Tbsp. mild chili powder and 1 Tbsp. brown sugar)
2 cups cooked rice
6 homemade corn tortillas
1 cup shredded cheddar cheese

In casserole dish, layer the rice first, then the chili.

Cut tortillas into quarters and quickly deep fry until crisp and puffy. Drain. Layer on top of chili and sprinkle with shredded cheese. Bake at 350° F until done. Serve with more tortilla chips and salsa.

Stews

Stews are filling, comforting, and pretty darned good, to boot. And, like casseroles, you can add or take away to suit your taste or use just what you have today. All this good food makes you forget that it's from your emergency pantry, doesn't it?

Brunswick stew

¼ cup bacon TVPs (textured soy protein)
1½ pints canned boneless chicken with liquid
1 qt. tomatoes
1 cup potatoes (cubed) or dehydrated equivalent
1 tsp. dehydrated onion powder
½ pint sliced celery
1 tsp. sugar
2 tsp. salt
half a lemon, sliced thin (or dehydrated equivalent)
1 tsp. black pepper
½ tsp. ground cloves
2 cups butter beans or sweet corn (or dehydrated equivalent)

Add all the ingredients in a large pot. Simmer gently until flavors blend well and serve.

This is a great leftover use-er-upper. You can use leftover holiday turkey instead of chicken. Throw in some carrots and tomatoes. The combination of poultry and tomatoes works well.

Venison stew

1 pint cubed, canned venison
¼ cup dehydrated onions or 2 large onions, quartered
1 qt. canned cut carrots or 3 large carrots, cut into chunks
1 pint sweet corn
1 tsp. dehydrated minced garlic or 1 large clove garlic, minced
1 qt. canned new potatoes or 4 medium potatoes, cubed
1 qt. tomato sauce
1 pint rutabagas, diced
1 tsp. salt
1 tsp. celery salt
2 tsp. black pepper

Combine all ingredients in a large, heavy stew pot, and heat slowly with lid on for 30 minutes (longer if fresh vegetables are used). When all ingredients are very tender, take off lid and slowly simmer until thick enough, but not scorched. Serve hot with thick slices of homemade bread or top with dumplings instead of cooking down further, place top on and cook for an additional 20 minutes until dumplings are fluffy and done.

Chicken chowder

2 Tbsp. butter
1 pint cubed, canned white boneless chicken meat
1 pint diced raw carrots or 1½ cups dehydrated
$^1/_8$ tsp. pepper
3 Tbsp. flour
1 Tbsp. dehydrated onion or ¼ cup chopped fresh
1 pint cubed canned potatoes or 1½ cups cubed raw potatoes
1 tsp. salt
2½ cups milk

Melt butter in heavy 3-quart saucepan. Add any raw vegetables with enough water to simmer until tender. Drain. Add cooked vegetables, chicken, seasonings together in saucepan. Add ½ cup milk and flour in a jar. Shake until blended well. Add this and remaining 2 cups of milk to the vegetable/chicken mixture. Cook over medium heat, stirring constantly until mixture thickens. We like this served with hot flour tortillas and homemade butter.

Meat pies

Although the very thought of eating store-bought "pot pies" gives me the willies, some of our favorite meals are flaky crusted, steaming pies of meat and vegetables. Tender crusted, they are quick to make and oh so good. They also make good use of rehydrated vegetables and leftover dabs of this and that. (I'll bet I can put together a "to die for" meat pie as fast as anyone can open four cardboard frozen imposters.)

I usually bake my meat pies in a medium cast iron frying pan, as we like lots of yummy filling. While you can use a bottom crust, I prefer a top crust only. It's quicker, and it's plenty of pastry.

Crust:

The crust for any of my meat pies is a basic fruit pie crust. I usually make a "double" batch of dough, as the crust for a meat pie is usually thicker and when I use a medium-sized cast iron frying pan, it is larger in diameter than a 9" pie tin.

Basic double pie crust

4 cups flour
1¾ cups shortening
enough ice water to make dough workable
1½ tsp. salt

Mix flour and salt, then cut in shortening until the size of peas; don't overwork. Add half a cup of ice water and mix. Add just enough more ice water to allow the dough to form a ball and be worked with; you don't want it sticky. Again, don't overwork or it will get tough. Form in a ball and chill if the day is warm. Roll out onto a floured surface to about a ¼ inch thick. Using a plate or other properly sized disc, cut the top crust of your meat pie. I usually cut steam slots in the top in the shape of two stems of wheat. It's pretty and lets steam out so the pie doesn't "grow bubbles." (Your crust should be just the size to fit snugly on

With dehydrated margarine and eggs, a recipe is always doable, even when chickens aren't laying and you don't have butter.

top of frying pan. I often cut them half an inch oversized and flute the edge, just for appearance, but you don't have to.)

The ingredients of the pie are mixed and put in the pan, then the top is placed carefully on. A hint: I carefully roll the crust up on my rolling pin and unroll it gently into place so it doesn't break up on me.

Turkey pot pie

2 Tbsp. butter
2 Tbsp. flour
2 cups milk
1 pint diced boneless turkey
1 cup canned carrots, sliced
1 Tbsp. dehydrated onion or 1 raw onion, chopped
¼ cup dehydrated peas
1 tsp. dehydrated green peppers
1 pint cubed canned potatoes or 2 large raw potatoes, cubed
crust (from recipe above)

In medium-sized cast iron frying pan, melt butter gently, stirring in flour to make roux. Add milk until your white sauce is medium thick; add more milk if necessary. Add the rest of ingredients and stir gently.

Top with crust. Bake at 350° F until crust is bubbly and light brown. It's great and quick to do, too.

Beef cowboy pie

2 Tbsp. butter
2 Tbsp. flour
1 pint tomato sauce
1 pint diced canned stewing beef
2 Tbsp. dehydrated onion or 2 medium raw onions, chopped
1 pint cubed canned potatoes
1 tsp. pepper
1 Tbsp. dehydrated beef stock soup base
1 tsp. chili powder
1 tsp. celery seed
crust from recipe above

Melt butter in heavy medium cast iron frying pan. Add flour, mixing well, then tomato sauce. If necessary, add just enough water to make a medium sauce. Add rest of ingredients, stirring gently. Top with crust and bake at 350° F until perfect.

Shepherd's pie

Shepherd's pie is a no-pastry meat pie and is one of our favorite quickies. The topping is browned mashed potatoes instead of a pastry. Give it a try. Folks will never believe it came from your storage food.

1 Tbsp. butter
1 qt. beef or venison meat slices
3 cups hot mashed potatoes (use dehydrated, reconstituted)
2 cups gravy (use meat juice,
water, flour, and soup base)

Generously butter bottom of medium cast iron frying pan. Spread mashed potatoes over bottom and up sides, about half inch thick. Layer sliced meat on top (I often add mushroom slices, too), topping it with the gravy. Top with a few spoonfuls of mashed potatoes over it, drizzling a little melted butter over them. Cover and bake at 350° F for about half an hour. You can add any vegetables to the meat before covering with gravy or top with cheese, powdered or grated, for ten minutes before taking out of the oven. This is an old-time standby.

Three very handy "goodies" from the storage pantry are dumplings, biscuits, and cornbread. All are great with stews and mixed dishes. Use them often and see how contented your "stuffed" family leaves the table!

Dumplings

1 cup flour
½ tsp. salt
2 tsp. baking powder
1 egg
$1/3$ cup melted butter
3 Tbsp. milk

Mix all dry ingredients and butter. Add egg and milk. Stir until just moistened. Drop by tablespoons into boiling gravy. Cover and simmer for 15-20 minutes. Do not remove cover until this time or they will fall flat! Serve at once when done. These dumplings will be tender and fluffy, just like Grandma's.

Corn bread

1 cup hot milk—dry, reconstituted   .
1 cup cornmeal
1 cup flour
$1/3$ cup honey
2 Tbsp. vegetable oil
1 egg
1 tsp. salt
3 tsp. baking powder

I use dry milk, reconstituted with boiling water, to mix with, first the cornmeal, then the rest of the ingredients. In this way, the cornbread is tender, and not as crumbly as it often is. I tried it and really like the difference. Mix the batter well and pour into a 9"x9" greased pan or a medium cast iron frying pan. Bake at 400° F about 20 minutes, until just done. I also often add a half pint of drained canned sweet corn and 1 tsp. mild chili powder for a Mexican style cornbread. Ole!

Biscuits

2 cups flour
½ cup shortening
1 tsp. salt
3 tsp. baking powder
1 cup milk or buttermilk

Mix flour and shortening until pieces are the size of a pea. Add salt and baking powder. Then mix in milk. If you use buttermilk, also add 1 tsp. baking soda. The dough should be moist, but dry enough to hold together for a brief kneading on a floured board. Pat down or roll out to about 1 inch thick and cut. I use a greased canning jar ring. Pat them a bit to fluff them up and place on a lightly greased cookie sheet. The biscuits should touch each other; this way they'll be tender and fluffy, not crunchy on the edges! Bake at 400° F until just golden on the edges. Serve hot with gravy or your favorite jam.

Along with these quick breads, you'll want to serve plenty of yeast rolls and breads of all types. There are so many possibilities, especially when you use an assortment of whole grains. We think of them as "special" breads—not "survival" foods! And with my breads and rolls, I constantly change my recipes a bit, adding a little of this or that, as the mood hits. For instance, I may toss in a handful of hulled sunflower

We recycle old tins for use as dry storage containers.

seeds, rolled oats, poppy seeds, ground dehydrated pumpkin (very good in whole wheat bread), or chopped nuts. I don't add enough to drastically alter a recipe, only spice it up a bit.

Prairie whole wheat bread

3 cups lukewarm liquid (potato water, milk, or water)

2½ Tbsp. dry yeast

1 cup warm water

2 beaten eggs

2 Tbsp. butter

1 cup cornmeal

2 tsp. salt

¼ cup honey

13 cups whole wheat flour

Heat liquid till very hot and remove from heat. Dissolve yeast in 1 cup warm water. When heated liquid is lukewarm, add 2 beaten eggs and softened butter. Add softened yeast. Add cornmeal and salt. Beat well. Then add honey, followed by flour, one cup at a time, mixing well between cups, until the dough is able to be turned out on a floured board to knead. Add extra flour, if necessary to make an elastic, yet moist dough. Knead well and place in a greased bowl, turning once to grease top. Cover with damp towel and let rise in warm place till doubled. Punch down and divide into 3 loaves and place in greased bread pans or cookie sheets for free-shaped loaves (braid 'em, for a fancy look). Again let rise and bake at 350° F, until tops are nicely browned. Take out of oven and grease tops with butter or margarine.

For an extra nice dinner, even in hard times, take the extra few minutes to make a pan of butter horns (crescent rolls) for the family. The ingredients aren't extraordinary, but the results are.

Butter horns

2 tsp. dry yeast
1 cup warm water
1 Tbsp. sugar
3 eggs, beaten
½ cup sugar
½ tsp. salt
½ cup shortening
5 cups white flour

Mix yeast, warm water, 1 Tbsp. sugar, and eggs in a mixing bowl and let stand 15 minutes. Then add ½ cup sugar, salt, shortening, and flour. Mix, then knead well. Place in greased, covered bowl and let stand in fridge overnight. Divide in 2 parts and roll out in 12 inch circles, cut into 16 wedges. Roll up, starting with the wide end. Let rise 3-4 hours. Bake at 400° F for 15 minutes. Brush with butter and serve piping hot.

Sometimes the thing we miss most in "survival" situations or just plain hard times is desserts! Maybe it's like when we were kids and were sad or sick, and Mom or Grandma fixed us something extra nice for dessert. Here are a few ideas that work well from the storage pantry.

Desserts

Oatmeal sunny cookies

1½ cups sifted flour
½ tsp. salt
1 tsp. baking powder
1 tsp. soda
2 cups brown sugar
1 cup shortening
2 eggs, beaten
1 tsp. vanilla
3 cups rolled oats
¾ cup sunflower seeds
powdered sugar

needed for my pantry

Sift flour, salt, baking powder, and soda. Cream sugar and shortening. Add beaten eggs and vanilla and beat well. Add dry ingredients and oats. Chill dough. Form into balls the size of a walnut. Roll in powdered sugar until heavily coated. Place 2 inches apart on greased cookie sheets. Put pecan in center of each, if desired. Press balls down. Bake at 375° F until just starting to brown.

Raised donuts

1 cup milk
½ cup sugar
1 tsp. salt
½ cup shortening
2 eggs, well beaten
1 Tbsp. dry yeast
3 ²/₃ cups flour

Scald milk. Add sugar, salt, and shortening. Let cool to lukewarm, then add eggs. Mix well. Then add yeast and let dissolve. Add flour and mix well. Let rise about 1 hour.

Punch dough and let rise again. Roll out dough on floured board and cut. If you don't have a donut cutter, cut in strips or use a wide mouth canning ring and another small cutter to cut out hole. Deep fry, then glaze or roll in granulated sugar.

Mock pecan pie

¼ cup butter or margarine
½ cup sugar
1 cup dark corn syrup
¼ tsp. salt
3 eggs, well beaten
½ cup coconut
½ cup quick rolled oats
9" unbaked pie crust

Cream butter, add sugar and corn syrup, mix till fluffy. Add salt, beat well. Add eggs, one at a time, beating well. Stir in coconut and oatmeal.

Pour into unbaked pie crust. Bake at 350° F. until knife inserted in center comes out clean. Cool before serving.

Fruit cobbler

2 Tbsp. margarine

2 cups sugar

3 cups flour

½ tsp. salt

3 tsp. baking powder

milk

drained, canned fruit

Soften margarine and mix with sugar, then add flour, salt, baking powder, and enough milk to make a cake batter. Pour a quart of drained home-canned fruit, such as blueberries, peaches, or pie cherries (If these have been canned without sugar or with a very light syrup, add ½ cup sugar to drained fruit.) into a baking dish. Top with batter. You can add nuts or raisins on top if you wish. Bake at 350° F 45-60 minutes or until crust is golden brown. Serve warm with sweetened cream or whipped cream. You'll forget these are hard times.

By now, you get the idea; just because the world (or your corner of it) is in turmoil, doesn't mean you have to suffer and eat boiled beans three meals a day. If you have your storage pantry, with at least a year—preferably two years' worth—of food available, you can eat well. Probably better than you are now! Rotating these foods by using them in your daily cooking assures that they remain fresh and nutritious.

You do not want to simply buy the touted "year's worth" of survival food and stash it under the bed and forget about it. By using these foods, you'll develop a knack for finding recipes your family loves. And by adding dozens and dozens of home-canned and dehydrated foods, as well as those from your garden, orchard, and homestead, you can eat very well. ❧

Other titles available from Backwoods Home Publications

The Best of the First Two Years
A Backwoods Home Anthology—The Third Year
A Backwoods Home Anthology—The Fourth Year
A Backwoods Home Anthology—The Fifth Year
A Backwoods Home Anthology—The Sixth Year
A Backwoods Home Anthology—The Seventh Year
A Backwoods Home Anthology—The Eighth Year
A Backwoods Home Anthology—The Ninth Year
A Backwoods Home Anthology—The Tenth Year
A Backwoods Home Anthology—The Eleventh Year
A Backwoods Home Anthology—The Twelfth Year
A Backwoods Home Anthology—The Thirteenth Year
A Backwoods Home Anthology—The Fourteenth Year
A Backwoods Home Anthology—The Fifteenth Year
A Backwoods Home Anthology—The Sixteenth Year
A Backwoods Home Anthology—The Seventeenth Year
A Backwoods Home Anthology—The Eighteenth Year
A Backwoods Home Anthology—The Nineteenth Year
A Backwoods Home Anthology—The Twentieth Year
A Backwoods Home Anthology—The Twenty-first Year
A Backwoods Home Anthology—The Twenty-second Year
A Backwoods Home Anthology—The Twenty-third Year
A Backwoods Home Anthology—The Twenty-fourth Year
A Backwoods Home Anthology—The Twenty-fifth Year
A Backwoods Home Anthology—The Twenty-sixth Year
A Backwoods Home Anthology—The Twenty-seventh Year
A Backwoods Home Anthology—The Twenty-eighth Year
A Backwoods Home Anthology—The Twenty-ninth Year